Informal Learning
in Youth Work

Informal Learning in Youth Work

Janet R. Batsleer

Los Angeles • London • New Delhi • Singapore

SAGE Publications Ltd
1 Oliver's Yard
55 City Road
London EC1Y 1SP

SAGE Publications Inc.
2455 Teller Road
Thousand Oaks, California 91320

SAGE Publications India Pvt Ltd
B 1/I 1 Mohan Cooperative Industrial Area
Mathura Road
New Delhi 110 044

SAGE Publications Asia-Pacific Pte Ltd
33 Pekin Street #02-01
Far East Square
Singapore 048763

Library of Congress Control Number: 2007932295

British Library Cataloguing in Publication data

A catalogue record for this book is available from the British Library

ISBN 978-1-4129-4618-6
ISBN 978-1-4129-4619-3 (pbk)

Typeset by Cepha Imaging Pvt. Ltd., Bangalore, India
Printed in India by Replika Press Pvt. Ltd
Printed on paper from sustainable resources

Contents

Acknowledgements

Thank you to colleagues and students at MMU who have offered support during the writing of this book.

An early version of Chapter 3 was presented to the Council of Europe Seminar on Young People and Social Exclusion in Budapest, November 2005.

Especially thank you to people who read work in draft: Bernard Davies, Mary Marken, Vera Martins, Rebecca O' Rourke, Carol Packham, Alison Ronan, John Shiers, Jean Spence, Diane Watt and to the anonymous reviewer for helpful feedback.

Margaret Beetham read the whole thing.

You are none of you responsible for any of the shortcomings.

Thank you to Julian and to Greg, and to Margaret. You know what for!

1

How to Use This Book

'Informal Education' is an educational practice which can occur in a number of settings, both institutional and non-institutional. It is a practice undertaken by committed practitioners. It may also be engaged in–at the margins of their activities–by other professionals, such as teachers, nurses and social workers. Most professional informal educators are not described in this way in job titles or job descriptions. Instead, job titles are associated with a particular client group. Common terms include: community education; community learning; lifelong learning; mentoring; social pedagogy; popular education; youth and community work; project work and youth engagement. The term 'non-formal learning' is also used in the context of European debates, as are the terms 'social pedagogue' and 'animateur', and these people engage in the same practice as youth and community workers. As I have been teaching for many years in the context of the professional training and education of youth and community workers, I refer interchangeably to youth and community workers, youth workers and informal educators.

This book addresses questions of power, recognition and redistribution indirectly but persistently. In particular, themes concerning gender, sexuality and race discrimination and social class will be found throughout the book and particularly draw on examples from urban contexts in which I have worked. These themes are interwoven in a framework in which informal learning as conversation is discussed.

Part One, 'Whose Agenda?' offers a framework for the social, political and personal reflection to be undertaken at the beginning of any informal education project. Part Two, 'Getting to Know Young People', follows the agenda set by Bernard Davies' *Youth Work: A Manifesto for Our Times* in addressing the questions: Who are these young people? Why are *they* here? Why are they *here*? (Davies, 2005). Part Three, 'Getting Deeper', explores a range of themes and contexts for informal learning which characteristically engage practitioners and young people once the initial periods of boundary-setting and testing-out is over. It might be called 'the middle period' of conversations, and is the heart of practice. The final part of the book, 'Unfinished Conversations' suggests some of the ways in which the practice of informal education overlaps with therapy on the one hand and community development and civic engagement on the other. These chapters enable reflection on the ways in which the everyday elements of informal learning have sometimes been implicated in profound personal social and political transformations. Each section ends with points for reflection for students and practitioners.

This book should not necessarily be read in order. It can be read by jumping about in it and finding the sections which hold the most interest for particular readers or on particular aspects of youth and community work training courses. The early chapters are rather more theoretical than many of the later ones and readers new to the subject of youth and community work might do better to read some of the later chapters first. Every chapter has a series of key points at the beginning and end and a set of suggestions for further reading which guide the reader, as well as examples from practice to reflect on. Some are long and accompanied by a commentary. Others are brief snapshots to spark ideas.

Part One: Whose Agenda?

The early chapters of the book concern work that needs to be undertaken at the beginning point of the cycle of engagement in youth and community work, and which will be returned to over and over again. Chapter 2 on 'Informal Learning and Informal Education' makes clear the basic understanding of youth work, conversation and empowerment which informs the book.

Chapter 3, 'Identity, Identity Politics and Rights', focuses attention on the significance of identity both as a theme of adolescence and as a highly politicised term which draws our attention to issues of power and the struggle for justice and recognition. This chapter offers an introduction to the subject of 'identity politics' and why it matters to youth and community work and an introduction to the idea of rights-based practice.

Chapter 4 on discourses of 'Social Inclusion and Exclusion' considers in depth the ways in which public policy–in particular social policy, education policy and criminal justice–has an impact on the work of youth and community workers. It offers a detailed analysis of how current policy discourses are operating. It encourages committed practitioners to take up a position of critical dialogue with those policies and offers some directions as to how this might be done.

Chapter 5 is concerned with reflective practice and how youth and community workers working in the context of diversity might use critical and reflective practice as a method for developing their work. This chapter presents an in-depth case study using the Johari window as a method of analysing the work of a diverse team of women educators working with Black young men.

Part Two: Getting to Know Young People

This section is concerned with what happens near the beginning of engagement in youth and community work.

Chapter 6, 'Understanding Young People', offers a discussion of some theoretical frameworks for understanding the term 'youth' and suggests ways in which youth workers need to consider the life stage and life context of the people they are working with as they begin the work. It offers a number of resources for doing this.

Chapter 7, 'Boundaries in Practice', discusses the meaning of this term both in the lives of young people and in the work of the professional youth and community worker, who very often has to establish professional boundaries and safe space for the work. This chapter also discusses the practice of 'positive action' in challenging boundaries which limit and restrict particular groups of young people.

Chapter 8, 'It's Boring…', is about some significant starting points for engaging youth work conversations. It offers examples of conversational repertoires, of starting points in discontent, dissatisfaction and disrespect. This chapter considers how youth and community workers respond to prejudice, put-downs and wind-ups among groups of young people.

Part Three: Getting Deeper

The chapters in this section are attempts to convey some of what happens once relationships are established and the informal learning is really happening.

Chapter 9 looks specifically at the creation of closed groups, particularly identity-based groups of various kinds–cultural groups, gender groups, faith groups, lesbian, gay, bisexual and trans groups–and explores possible rationales for such groups and the ways youth and community workers have developed them.

Chapter 10 considers the importance of voluntary relationship in informal learning and the nature of the relationship between the youth worker and young person as a source for learning about other aspects of negotiation, agency and competence in adult life. Youth work as a practice of accompaniment and of respectful relationship is discussed in this chapter.

Chapter 11 is concerned with the role of friendship in the practice of youth and community work. The question of professionalism and the nature and purpose of professional boundaries is also discussed here.

Chapter 12 develops the theme of the work of youth and community workers as 'animateurs' by focusing specifically on the role of imagination and creativity (rooted in play) in practice and drawing on examples and case studies from arts-based work.

Part Four: Unfinished Conversations

In the final section, the book opens up discussion of directions in which both youth and community workers and young people may be led, which may go beyond some of the limits of professional practice and engage in wider conversations, both personal and political.

Chapter 13 considers the experience of silencing and being silenced in conversation. It focuses on youth work responses to bullying, to anger and self-destructive behaviour, to attempted suicide and to death and loss.

Chapter 14 explores the theme of silence from the other side: as a place of solitude, solidarity and delight. This chapter considers the place of outdoor education in youth work as well as offering insights into the contribution of models of spiritual development to youth work practice. It investigates the difference between loneliness and solitude, and the place of faith-based practice.

Chapter 15 explores the theme of democracy and participation and suggests that the models of citizenship and citizen participation on which youth workers may draw are highly contested. Nevertheless, the opportunity to make the links between the personal and political, the local and the global is significant and is offered to youth workers by participation programmes.

Chapter 16 investigates the politics of 'community cohesion' and offers a number of alternative models drawn from international contexts for ways of exploring the issues of commonality and difference in communities divided by histories of migration, of racism and of war.

2

Informal Learning and Informal Education

- Learning through conversation and through dialogue as the most important method of informal learning.
- Empowerment. What is power? How do informal educators engage with power dynamics and conflicts?
- Respectful conversation. How can we treat those we work with 'as equals' and 'with mutual respect' in situations of practical inequality?
- Why youth work? Working with people who are young gives a particular focus to informal learning: the transition from childhood to adulthood.

What is informal learning?

Youth and community work is about dialogue, about conversation. What do youth and community workers do? Listen and talk. Make relationships. Enable young people to come to voice. 'Conversation' conveys a sense of the mutual learning which the practice at its best enables. The roles of educator and learner are each present in informal education. One of the purposes of this book is to sharpen understanding of the work of the professional informal educator (Smith, 1988).

Informal educators, youth and community workers, go to meet people and start where those people are with their own preoccupations and in their own places. In informal education, both learner and educator engage in a process of learning from the context of the everyday. In a shared engagement with everyday problem-posing, new learning occurs. It occurs because the learning is of immediate significance to those involved, rather than derived from a pre-established curriculum. The primary role of the youth and community worker is to act as a facilitator of learning.

There are significant differences between the subject-based curriculum of formal learning and learning which occurs in the process of informal education–learning, for example, about identity, about others and our relationships with them, about relationships with the wider world and the contexts of our lives. There are of course overlaps, especially with citizenship education, with religious education, with sport, with personal and health education, with drama and all the arts. But the point of engagement between the educator and young people is not the body of knowledge: it is the development of the young people themselves and of their life-world.

There are major differences between the processes of assessment appropriate to formal education and those which are appropriate to informal education. There has been a renewed emphasis in recent years on the importance of the recognition of learning in the processes of informal education. Enabling the recognition of learning, watching for 'the penny to drop' and listening for signs of 'moving on' is a significant element of practice. Youth workers look out for those moments in the conversation, as it develops, when something clicks, when something has been achieved, so that learning is acknowledged and recognised.

There has been vigorous debate about the accreditation of informal learning and the use of certification in this setting (Miles et al., 2002; Ord, 2007). Accreditation of the outcomes of informal education is a funding requirement across much of the sector in the United Kingdom, with much of adult education and youth work required to produce 'accredited outcomes'. The Duke of Edinburgh Awards, ASDAN Awards (for accreditation of personal development) and a range of other schemes of accreditation are a necessary part of the youth and community worker's 'toolkit'. This is a mixed blessing. Whilst it is hard to deny the satisfaction that both workers and young people feel when their work together is recognised by the award of a certificate, the focus on assessment which is the basis of awarding accreditation threatens to limit informal education and perversely to lower expectations of what can be achieved in the process (Brent, 2004). Recognition of development through informal learning opportunities as distinct from the accreditation of informal learning is therefore the focus in this book.

Informal education can occur with people of any age. The focus in this book is on **young people** as participants in informal education. In the (over-)developed world, participation in formal education, and then the transition from school to the labour market through a variety of further and higher education opportunities, marks the life stage between the ages of 14 and 21. There is significant evidence that the adolescent transition has become extended even further, continuing into the mid-twenties, partly as a result of the policies that have extended educational opportunities and restructured the labour market (Catan, 2004). Most young people remain economically dependent on their families or else on loans or on benefit payments well into their twenties. This in turn affects housing transitions and the age at which families are started. Such transitions are now happening over an extended period, and young people might therefore reasonably look for greater support. The link between informal learning as collaborative enquiry and informal learning as a process of informal support is inescapable in youth work. Conversation, as the basis of practice, links young people's personal agendas with wider social and political agendas, and forms the bond between informal learning and informal support in the practice.

Conversation and dialogue

Conversation, in the sense used here, is more than chat. Conversation is a series of exchanges between two or more people over time through which meaning and understanding are deepened. It is an art rather than a technique or a science, but it is an art which enables a 'going deeper', a development of knowledge and understanding and a growing encounter with truthfulness. Youth and community work as a practice is about making and developing a sense of meaning with young people, based on increasing commitment to searching out truthful information and understandings.

It does not rest content with the repetition or circulation of received prejudices or other everyday 'common sense' ideas. Conversation is a vehicle of enquiry, which opens up new ideas and new ways of understanding the world, to free those involved in the conversations from the manipulations of the powerful. In particular, it seeks, through education, to help people to understand how our desires and feelings are shaped and manipulated and to explore alternative and sometimes hidden desires. Conversation, or dialogue, contrasts with monologue, historically the major form of speech or instruction in schooling.

An anti-conversational model of education looks something like this. The teacher speaks according to a set curriculum which must be ingested by the student. The teacher distributes handouts, or requires a certain pattern of response to guidelines. The students listen, read and take notes. The teacher sets an examination, or offers pro-forma guidance for self-assessment. The students aim to reproduce accurately what they have learned in a written examination, and to meet the teacher's expectations for their personal portfolios. Such a process was memorably described by the great educationalist Paolo Freire as a 'banking' model of education, in which educators deposit knowledge in the empty vaults of students' minds. The model of education as dialogue is an ancient one, which Freire retrieved in his paradigmatic work. Education as dialogue, as critical dialogue, is the paradigm for all the discussions in this book. (Freire, 1972). Informal education as conversation should never be a monologue or even a series of 'yes' and 'no' replies to leading questions.

Conversation cannot be coerced, but it can be anticipated. The role of the informal educator cannot be taken for granted in the way that the role of a teacher in a classroom can be taken for granted. The youth worker's role has to be acknowledged and negotiated with the people with whom they are working. If it is not acknowledged, there can be no youth work. Conversation really cannot be required. It is engaged in freely, when people are interested and involved in a topic because they feel it matters. Equally, it is disengaged from freely. We switch off when we are bored, when the topic of conversation no longer engages us, perhaps when someone else's agenda becomes so dominating that others' including our own, become lost.

Conversation is made up of speaking and listening. The 'turn-taking' of roles as speaker and as listener, the increasing coming to voice of young people, replace the patterns of dominance, manipulation and silence encouraged by monologic 'banking' practices in education. When conversation is going well, we can say that conversation flows. This flow of conversation can enable creative engagement with conflict. Conflict is a major aspect of the lives of many young people, whether conflict within the family or on a wider community or even global scale. The flow of conversation can break down when conflicts happen: conversation can be silenced and stop flowing altogether as a means of conflict avoidance. Conversation involves mutuality and exchange and these conditions are easily destroyed. However, conflict need not silence or destroy the conditions for conversation. Part of the role of the informal educator is to keep the conditions for conversation alive, even in situations of conflict.

Conversational repertoires, registers and themes

In the course of conversation, there are a number of conversational repertoires and registers and themes. By conversational repertoires, I mean clusters of topics or themes and ways of engaging with them. This forms the substance of what has been called the curriculum of informal education. There has been a great deal of discussion of the 'curriculum' of youth and community work (Ord, 2007). Adopting a 'curriculum model' brings the practice close to engagement and contrasts with formal education and assessment. Instead, this book is concerned with the identification of 'generative themes'. These themes are always situated in specific contexts: the specific local contexts and historical moments of the groups with whom youth and community workers engage. The term 'generative themes' (Freire, 1972) refers simply to the 'life-giving' or 'life-enhancing' quality of the repertoire of conversation in which informal educators engage. The themes emerge from the realities of the participants in conversation.

Conversational registers are the tones and colours of conversations, the kind of language used, whether they are 'street' conversations or 'formal' conversations, 'parental' conversations or the conversations of 'street mates', boasting or inspiring conversations, humorous conversations full of jokes and banter and backchat, private and personal listening, story-telling and mysterious talk late at night round a fire, talk based on bragging rights or chat-up lines, praise and astonishment, talk full of admonishing, advising, proverbs, folk wisdom or chastisement. All of these happen in youth work.

Since language is the main vehicle of conversation, committed practitioners need to have a keen awareness of language and talk, its different registers and tones and the nature of communication in talk. All youth and community workers need to strive to be bilingual at least–able to engage in particular local talk and also in the formal languages of education and the wider society.

Starting points in informal education are the conscious decisions about which conversations to join and enter into, in the complex web of conversations that are going on. In the flow of speaking and listening, as conversation moves from chat to more serious talk, languages develop and change, are critiqued, mocked, undermined, embellished, deepened. Meanings and understandings change. Conversation is a form of sociality and of bridge-building. Talk can also be the ground of non-communication, mistrust and gathering mutual suspicion. Conversation carries feelings along with meanings, and the feelings form part of meanings. Conversation sometimes accompanies or instigates actions.

Empowerment

Informal educators need to recognise conversation as part of a process of empowerment, which also includes actions. Through conversation, groups of people may be enabled to discover what is within their grasp and what is outside their power, to ask questions, through collaborative investigation, about the limits that have been set for them and their lives. People may begin to challenge the limits that appear to have been set for them and, in so doing, to change them. 'Never underestimate the ability of a small group of committed citizens to change the world,' as the anthropologist Margaret Mead is alleged to have said: 'indeed it is the only thing that ever has.'

This is the tradition of democratic political education, including feminist group-work practice, which is a source of much that has been creative in youth and community work. This book aims to build on the work of Tony Jeffs and Mark Smith (Jeffs and Smith, 1988; Smith, 1993; Jeffs and Smith, 1996a). Smith's work distanced itself to some extent from the engagement with questions of power and oppression which characterised the understanding of informal education as it developed from the work of Paolo Freire in the 1970s (Smith, 1993). It is time to reconnect the account of conversation in informal education with the themes of power, conflict, inequality and difference.

Without such attention and reconnection with discussions of power and empowerment, the idea of conversation floats free from the reality of the pushing, shoving, joshing banter of everyday talk. The sparks, the power-charged moments of conversations are lost. Sparks fly in conversation and understandings shift and change. Just as often, misunderstandings deepen, anger or contempt is expressed. And, when the sparks fly, new groupings emerge, new connections are made, new separations happen, and new movement and new energies are released. It is in part through this process that power relations shift and are transformed.

'Empowerment' in informal learning happens as a result of such conversations. Its meaning is connected to 'education for liberation', in the sense of freedom from false and constraining understandings and contexts. Of course, 'empowerment' is not only small scale and interpersonal. It frequently refers to and requires large-scale movements and large-scale, global change. It has sometimes been the privilege of those involved in informal education to be touched by and involved in such transformations, as was the case for those involved in feminist education projects, in workers' education movements and in anti-colonial education movements.

Many committed practitioners have turned away from accounts of informal education practice as empowerment because of the implication–and the term is frequently used in practice settings–that empowerment is something which professionals do *to* clients, young people, service users. It may be true that 'to talk of empowering people is to risk being anti-liberatory. At worst, it encourages dependency of the empowered on the empowerer and a view of people as objects to be acted on. It can also obscure the nature of the processes involved. Power is a feature of relationships. It is not something gifted or given' (Jeffs and Smith, 1996a: 16).

Or else empowerment is seen as a commodity to be gained at the end of education. The idea that 'knowledge is power' has been changed to mean something like 'qualifications give access to status'. Others have rejected the term 'empowerment' because it has, particularly in a number of health and social care contexts, become coterminous with 'customer choice'. It seems to have lost its democratic and collective moorings and to refer only to individual choices about services.

The fact that such interpretations of the term 'empowerment' exist should not lead informal educators to abandon the analysis of power relationships as part of their praxis. Rather the reverse. It should lead us to engage in a closer analysis of power relationships and their impact on practice, as a prerequisite of the work we undertake. Conversations which occur without a sense of the power dynamics within which they are occurring frequently break down. Ignoring the analysis of power means failing to recognise the ways in which power dynamics might shift in order to benefit young people.

Empowerment is not something gifted or given to others. It is a term best used in the context of self-activity and mutual aid, and in the recognition that power gained through conversation is not a matter of only giving or taking, but rather a matter of give-and-take. Many activists in political movements have argued that power is always taken, never given, and never given up without a fight. 'Power concedes nothing without a demand. It never did and it never will,' said Frederick Douglass, the former slave. Yet there *are* moments of concession when existing power relationships shift. Something is given away or abandoned, if not generously gifted to another. A new freedom is taken and enjoyed.

Discussion Point

If there is no struggle, there is no progress. Those who profess to favor freedom and yet depreciate agitation .... want crops without plowing up the ground, they want rain without thunder and lightning. They want the ocean without the awful roar of its many waters .... Power concedes nothing without a demand. It never did and it never will. (Frederick Douglass, Abolitionist Orator, 1857)

What power struggles are affecting youth and community work today?

Whether this is on a large scale–such as the abandonment of the practice of slave-owning or the abandonment of the male monopoly on voting–or on a very small scale, such as the offering of a place on a local area partnership network or a parish council to young people, shifts in power dynamics do involve a 'give' and 'take'. Indeed who does the giving and who the taking is very often precisely what is being fought over.

In situations where there is no power balance and where there is clear inequality, there are almost always conflicts of interest. It may sometimes be for the best if the acting out of those conflicts of interest can be avoided but it is not usually sensible for their existence to be denied in the name of some ideological claim to 'unity' or 'cohesion'. Sometimes, the creative way forward in a conversation is for a clash of interests and perspectives to be made visible. The naming of a conflict enables development to happen which had previously been blocked. Failure to engage with a clash of interests means that an opportunity to open up to new horizons of conversation and to new development is missed, whether personally, within a small group or within a particular community.

Empowerment, alliance and respectful conversations

Smith (1993: 158) suggests that promoting dialogue is problematic in the context of a model of education as struggle. 'Can dialogue occur between those who want to name the world and those who do not want this naming; or between those who have been denied the right to speak and those who deny the right?' Asked bluntly in this way, it is hard to see where engagement in conversation can happen. But only in some extreme situations are people entirely voiceless even when others ignore or wish to silence them. 'There is no such thing as the voiceless,' said the Indian campaigner and novelist Arundhati Roy: 'there are only the silenced and the deliberately misheard' (Roy, 2002).

The conversation which matters for informal educators may not be the dialogue 'between those who name the world and those who do not want this naming', but rather the conversation *among* 'those who do not want this naming' and their allies concerning the question of what better names there are. The theme of working coalitions, of alliances and conversations across difference, is an important theme of this book. Conversation may be conceived as a process of coming to voice, and then of using that voice to investigate and explore reality, in a collaborative rather than competitive way. This means engaging with the names that have been assigned to us and with the ways that our realities have been described. A process of accepting, modifying and rejecting those namings occurs continually. When the conversation moves on from chat to more serious talk, informal education is a part of that power-charged process. This means that there are times when the informal educator makes choices and pursues a conversation in one place rather than another or with one group and not another.

It is wrong to suggest that a conversation cannot occur where conflict exists. However, such conversations are inevitably highly charged. Educators need therefore to be prepared to work in the presence of strong emotions, including love/hate and grief/anger/fear. Particular kinds of conversation are possible where conflict is mediated. At times this book may seem to be preoccupied with issues of hurt, violence and conflict. I explicitly repudiate any suggestion that the groups with whom youth and community workers engage are inevitably more violent or prejudiced or conflict-ridden than other, usually more affluent, social groups. But neither do I believe that practice is well served by avoiding discussions of conflict and violence.

Not all conflict can be mediated. Equally, not all power imbalance or inequality results in immediate conflict. The notion of a respectful conversation which can mitigate the effects of inequality is one which has gained considerable currency. The term 'accompaniment' can be usefully placed alongside 'dialogue' as a conceptualisation of the work of informal educators, particularly the work of adults with young people. Maxine Green and Chandu Christian developed the use of the term in their work on informal education and spiritual development (Green and Christian, 1998), suggesting an analogy with the relationship between singer and accompanist. The image has been used beautifully by Richard Sennett.

Discussion Point

Respect is an expressive performance. That is, treating others with respect doesn't just happen, even with the best will in the world: to convey respect means finding the words and gestures which make it felt and convincing. Just as Fisher-Dieskau performs respect for his pianist Gerald Moore, so does, I think, the professional youth worker who learns to criticise homeless adolescents without turning them off. (Sennett, 2003: 167)

When were you last challenged and still felt respected? How did that happen?

Such respectful conversations are the threads of a woven cloth. The cloth is the community that holds and sustains us, locally and globally.

Young

Youth workers work with young people ... because they are young. (Davies, 2005)

Informal education with young people is a method of offering support to the rising generation, of enabling them to take up the opportunities to become creators not consumers of their society and their world. Youth work as informal support engages with the social situation of young people, their rights and needs, and also with their emotions and personal development. Contemporary sociological accounts of 'youth' inform this book, as do accounts of the significance of emotional engagement and of unconscious and partially conscious processes in education and in the formation of youthful identities. Understanding identity formation as an aspect of adolescence is fundamental.

Models of development enable educators to consider the forms of engagement in learning which make sense in relation to the age of learners. The learning through play in which children characteristically engage never quite disappears but for most adults it has ceased to be the dominant form of learning. Adolescents are by definition no longer children and not yet adults. Imagination has a particularly significant part to play in development at this stage in life, as separation from parents or parent figures happens. This separation, produced in the transition to adult life, can be termed a 'separation crisis'. The process of separation and identity formation is marked by a new set of attachments to a peer group among whom new constructions of identity can be explored.

Theorists of young transitions suggest that this is a period of life when creativity and imagination may be at their height, and that music, style and 'youth cultures' have a particular importance in the process of identity-formation. Informal educators who engage with people at this stage of life have an enormous responsibility to recognise the 'not yet adult' place from which young people can engage.

Key Terms

'**Coming to voice**' and '**breaking the silence**' are important ideas throughout this book. They draw on a tradition of critical and emancipatory pedagogy.

Empowerment as a basis for informal learning is also explored throughout this book. The conceptualisation of social pedagogy and social education as **informal learning** was developed particularly in the UK in the 1980s. In the European, and also in the Welsh context, the term **non-formal learning** is more commonly used.

Further Reading

Freire, P. (1972) *Pedagogy of the Oppressed*. Harmondsworth: Penguin. This text offers a foundation for the pedagogical ideas found in this book.

hooks, b. (1994) *Teaching to Transgress: Education as the Practice of Freedom.* London and New York: Routledge. Hooks builds on Freire's work and embraces an engaged pedagogy at ease with diversity.

Smith, M.K. (1993) *Local Education: Community, Conversation, Praxis.* Maidenhead: Open University Press. Together with Tony Jeffs, Mark Smith has firmly located youth and community work as an educational, conversational and associational praxis.

Part I

Whose Agenda?

3

Identity, Identity Politics and Rights

- Identity matters to all young people, perhaps especially to young people positioned as marginalised or deviant.
- Identities sometimes influence the unequal allocation of opportunities and resources.
- Some identities are valued and others are devalued.
- All identities are complex, inescapably plural and have aspects that are silenced and can be brought to voice through informal education.
- Rights-based practice offers an ethical basis for responding to identity politics.

Who am I? Where do I belong in the world? Youth workers become very familiar with the struggles young people face in developing a sense of identity.

The transition to adulthood is a period of exploring and trying on the forms of adult identity that seem to be on offer to us, as well as a process of questioning and challenging them. This time of our lives is of great significance as we move towards the establishment of a secure adult ego, or 'identity'.

For some young people, the period of negotiation of adult identities is a period of intense struggle, especially if their emerging identities do not conform to adult expectations or to widely accepted norms. The claims for the theme of 'identity' as a basis for informal education practice with young people have been most strongly made from the perspective of communities who have been marginalised. When people are positioned as 'deviants' or 'outsiders', the question of the meanings of identity becomes a power struggle. Feminists dissatisfied both with the constructions of adult femininity available to them and with the value assigned to femininity in a masculine-dominant culture have instigated collaborative enquiries into and changes in the meanings of adult womanhood. Gay, lesbian and, increasingly, bisexual and transgendered people have challenged first the invisibility and then the stigmatising of homosexual identities as abnormal or unnatural. Black psychologists and psychotherapists have examined the impact of white racism on the identity-formation processes of Black young people, or young people of colour. The 'othering' (marking out as 'different') of Jewishness and of Islam in Christian culture marks the identity of Jewish and Muslim peoples, as well as the identity of Christians, in ways that construct both Jews and Muslims as 'outsiders within'. Disabled young people are constructed as 'special needs cases' and rendered outsiders as a result.

The significance and complexity of identity is also recognised in cultural and psychoanalytic theories, which suggest that all identities are formed in contradiction and conflict, both psychic and social. No one's identity is either singular or uncontradictory. Identity is always created out of a sense of commonality with and difference from others, out of identification and dis-identification. These patterns, in which we are caught up from birth, are the relations through which both our sense of our gender and our sexualities are formed. They are highly complex, contradictory and personal.

Identity politics

It is not only at the level of personal meaning-making that identities matter. The term 'identity politics' suggests the society-wide power struggles that are at stake. The phrase has been widely used to refer to the new social movements which blossomed in what was termed the New Left of the 1960s and 1970s and which unsettled older assumptions about progressive politics: movements such as Black Power, the Gay Liberation Front, the Women's Liberation Movement, Disabled People's Rights activism. Earlier progressive movements had assumed that the pursuit of the economic and social interests of the working class was the key driver of social change and social progress. As well as continuing to pursue social justice, the new movements emphasised the importance of consciousness in securing existing power relationships and keeping the system going, as well as in critical education for change.

Identity and self-naming

In the context of a politics of liberation which saw power as exercised through ideological controls, changes in consciousness were seen as a necessary condition for the transformation of society. 'Consciousness-raising' as a practice was particularly important in the politics of new social movements. For example, until the 1960s it was widely taken for granted that an employer could take family responsibilities of men into account when offering jobs and wages, and at the same time could refuse to appoint women because they were pregnant or had children. Consciousness-raising about the attitudes that underpinned such an approach to employment was supported by campaigning and activism which eventually brought about a change in the law: the Equal Pay and Sex Discrimination Acts.

Everyday consciousness, in which we live out our relationships, is not a sufficient basis for understanding ourselves, our conditions of life and the power relationships that sustain them. It is 'social cement' for the maintenance of existing social relationships but it does not produce energy for change. Everyday consciousness, or 'magical consciousness' to use Freire's term, tends to view the way things are as predetermined, set by fate, as out of control and unalterable as the way that night follows day (Freire, 1972). Received ideas about what it means to take on a particular social identity—what it means to be a man or a woman, what it means to be 'Asian' or 'Muslim', what it means to be 'Christian', what it means to come from a poor neighbourhood—are lived as if they were inevitable, natural and normal.

Informal education conversations can challenge these taken-for-granted convictions about the everyday. In this, they share in the capacity of all genuine education to unsettle, and 'wake up'. In so doing, they may very well unsettle the existing patterns of relationship in a family, wider community or neighbourhood. All education can be life-changing.

The fact that it can be so produces difficult ethical dilemmas for educators whose work seems to provoke these changes. Consciousness-raising work, which involves increasing awareness of one's own situation, very often extends to a development of political consciousness and awareness of the links between one's own predicaments and the politics of the wider world. All education which is critical participates in a fundamental human stance of wonder, amazement and curiosity about the world.

Identity: conflicts and divisions

In the post-colonial and anti-colonial context, educators inspired by the work of Franz Fanon (1986) and Alberto Memmi (1965) recognised the significance of enabling people whose communities and experiences had been colonised to name their own reality. Such a commitment to speaking in our own tongues and in our own voices rather than in the language of colonisers remains an essential moment in self-recovery and consciousness-raising, even when the nature of the mother tongue or authentic language shifts and changes. The ability to understand the nature of internalised oppression, the ways in which identities may be constructed by taking on the discourse of the coloniser, is an important resource for youth and community workers aiming to develop consciousness-raising conversations.

Black educators have pointed to the existence of a 'double consciousness' in their communities: a consciousness which is constructed by the racist or colonial designations of identity, and a consciousness which resists this. The use of screensavers depicting the 9/11 attacks on the Twin Towers, and pictures of Bin Laden as signatures on mobile phones may be current examples of such double consciousness. It might be understood as saying: 'If you see me as a terrorist, I will appear to confirm that I am one. I will confirm (and also parody) the fears that you project on to me.'

The aim of consciousness-raising conversation is to enable people to gain their voice and to enable aspects of the self that may usually be silenced to emerge. It encourages people to name their own realities rather than simply adapt to the ways in which their realities are named for them. For example, it was as a result of resistance to all the derogatory meanings and uses of the term 'Blacks' to refer to African-American people that the 'Black is Beautiful' movement emerged. Islamic youth work is emerging as a movement in a similar context. Muslim is a name with which young people are currently choosing to identify. The more the name Muslim is denigrated, and associated with 'Taliban' or 'terrorism', the more young people will seek to challenge this and create a new, positive and alternative set of meanings. 'Muslim youth work' is being developed in the context of informal education conversations which enable the questioning of received ideas and official scripts.

Hence the slogan of the Muslim Youth Work Foundation: 'Responding to lives not events (Khan, 2006).

Identity and the politics of redistribution

The politics of identity is also concerned with power in the distribution of resources. For most people–although not for some: for example those who are described as people with learning disabilities–the transition to adulthood is a transition from the relative powerlessness and the unique forms of power of infancy and childhood to the powers and competences of adult life.

However, the powers of adult life are not shared equally or distributed democratically and adolescent constructions of identity are linked to the social distribution of adult powers. 'Identity politics' can be understood as a struggle over the distribution of those powers and resources, concerned with issues of fairness and the possibility of redistributive justice.

It's not fair that boys are allowed out and girls are not, or that so many young disabled people do not access leisure opportunities with their able-bodied peers. It's not fair that the minimum wage is lower for young people than for adults. It's not fair that the police stop and search so many more young Black men than young white men. Gender identity still marks segregated labour markets and unequal pay. Some aspects of identity in contemporary societies are conduits through which resources of time, money and opportunities are implicitly allocated and distributed. Many people whose primary concern is with fairness and non-discrimination will argue that such matters as gender, 'race', sexuality and ability/disability should be irrelevant when allocating opportunities or rewards. They would like to see such identities cease to matter. This perspective is in tension with another way of understanding the significance of identity to politics: the politics of recognition.

Identity and the politics of recognition

The politics of recognition is concerned with invisibility, stigma and denigration, the dehumanising of whole populations on the basis of their identity. 'Don't be a big girl's blouse' (said to anyone who lacks courage); 'Look out! Here's the Taliban' (said to any young Muslim with a beard); 'You're gay' (routine insult to suggest that someone is strange or a misfit): these are current examples of such denigration.

Discussion Point

Stereotype: reduces a complex and plural identity to a single feature and makes a complex human being stand as a cipher for a group. Creates a 'black and white design' and facilitates an 'us and them' relationship.

List as many stereotypes as you can that affect the people you work with. How can they be understood, using this definition?

Such group stereotypes are highly significant in the marking of boundaries between 'us' and 'them', along which so much contemporary conflict moves. The difference between Muslims and 'the West' is one powerful construction of difference. Another is that between the South and the North: a difference represented by the presence of refugees as well as by global anti-poverty campaigns. In all these polarisations, the affirmation of a particular loved 'us' can turn on the construction of a hated 'them'. Such global polarisations draw the map, form the conditions in which young people negotiate identities and their sense of being and belonging in the world. Each side in the conflict projects negative identities on to the others. My 'terrorist' is your 'freedom fighter'. To engage in the politics of recognition means to challenge invisibility and to seek out positive affirmation of despised identities.

Those who seek non-discrimination and fairness may wish the categories of identity to cease to matter or cease being referred to in the allocation of resources. Those engaged in the politics of recognition may well wish to see hitherto stigmatised identities affirmed: Black is Beautiful, Muslim is European. 'All Different, All Equal' is the name of an important Council of Europe youth campaign against racism and xenophobia. In pursuit of equality and fairness, we may wish identities to matter less and less. In pursuit of self-respect and the acceptance of diversity, we may wish our identities to be celebrated and recognised.

The influence of these new social movements associated with 'identity politics' has extended through public and professional life. Most codes of professional ethics in education and social care now embrace a commitment to non-discrimination, and to 'anti-oppressive practice'. For youth workers, this engagement with issues of social justice, drawing on methods of collaborative enquiry, including consciousness-raising, has been a key element in the professional commitment to challenge discrimination and exclusion.

Rights-based practice

A rights-based approach to practice has afforded a strong ethical basis to such work (Crimmens and Whalen, 1999). Rather than *starting* from an assessment of young people's lives and contexts in terms of their needs and what they lack (a deficit model) or from the standpoint of crisis interventions which may make young people seem inherently problematic (a pathologising model), informal education starts from assumptions about the potential and capacities of young people and their rights to develop those capacities. These capacities are believed to be inherent to all human life and human agency and to be the ground of *equal* moral rights to freedom and well-being. According to Amartya Sen and Martha Nussbaum, such an understanding of human capacities forms the basis of our claims to rights. The language of human rights allows us to think about our rights to develop capabilities which we exercise freely. A capability is 'a person's ability to do valuable acts or to achieve valuable states of being'. Our well-being is therefore measured by our capability to do or be what we have reason to value. Statements of rights, in this context, are one way of stating 'what we have reason to value' (Nussbaum and Sen; 1993; Nussbaum, 1999; Sen, 1999).

There are a number of important international declarations of rights that inform practice: the United Nations Declaration on Human Rights and the United Nations Declaration on the Rights of the Child are the most significant. Much social struggle has arisen from the experience of people who have felt themselves excluded from legal and judicial and political declarations of rights and therefore, in some way, from the human community. This has been true of trade unionists, of women, of slaves and former slaves, of lesbians and gay men and of children, to name just some of the most significant groups who have needed to organise and struggle to claim rights. They have needed to organise movements to claim rights even in democratic societies which believed they were treating and declaring all equal. Claims to identity, claims to community and claims to rights are very closely associated. This is particularly clear in the changing legal status of the gay community. Having successfully claimed gay identity as identity rather than 'deviant' or 'pathological behaviour', gay people have in consequence been successful in achieving a measure of equal rights and fair treatment, as well as recognition within the law.

The United Nations Declaration on Human Rights and the United Nations Declaration on the Rights of the Child have been strengthened by further declarations, such as the Fourth United Nations World Conference on Women, which placed particular emphasis on the full human rights of the girl child: this is known as the Beijing Declaration. It gave the following focuses to projects across the world:

- Right to life
- Right to education
- Political rights
- Right to paid employment
- Contraception/Family planning
- Life free of torture and violence
- Consent to marriage
- Adequate nutrition and health

Once such declarations are made, governments are invited to become signatories and to develop legislation which supports the principles outlined. In this way international declarations influence change at national and local level. Such declarations reinforce development projects internationally, offering a starting point. Projects have emerged which reflect a shift in perception of young women's and young men's role in the world.

The themes of such declarations arise again and again in informal education. They always present ethical dilemmas. The following example gives an indication of some of the challenges facing practitioners focusing on the right to live free from violence, a right enshrined in all declarations. In focusing on 'rights', their practice inevitably draws attention to issues of power and of relationship.

Case Study

A youth worker takes up a post at a youth project in which, in the view of the newly appointed worker, the relationship between some older young men who use the project and some of the girls takes the form of sexual exploitation. The professional code of ethics on which the youth worker's intervention is based makes it essential for them not to ignore their perceptions. What form does the conversation take with the young men and the young women? How is consciousness raised in the process?

The young people concerned are reluctant to engage directly in a conversation about what is happening in their mixed urban neighbourhood. There are some girls–and they could be from any of the communities in the neighbourhood–who have grown up in families in which domestic violence has been tolerated. They have then themselves formed relationships in which regular violence has played a significant part. Some boys and girls come from families in the local Pakistani heritage community in which marriage and consent to marriage remains a contested issue. Most of the young men and women using the project–whether from white British, or Pakistani-heritage backgrounds–do not have any significant immediate experience of family violence and coercion.

The new worker first creates a safe space in which the young women can be together and can talk about their feelings. The focus of the work is the build-up to a series of community-based activities to celebrate International Women's Day. All of these enjoyable activities create an assumption that women have a right to the space of the youth centre. Dance events, fashion sessions, art events, cookery: these traditionally female-oriented activities are used by the staff to build up confidence in themselves and in one another.

Meanwhile, another member of the staff team begins an assertive conversation with the young men involved about the acceptability and the possible illegality of their activities with the young women. The staff recognise that it is important that both young men and young women are involved in this conversation. Some young men choose to leave the project as a result of the conversation. Others recognise the need to change their behaviour and stay involved. A discussion about what makes for good relationships between men and women develops.

The confidence-building work being undertaken is potentially affirming for the majority of young men and young women, who do not see violence or coercion as an acceptable basis for relationships. It may also be very unsettling. Young women at risk of forming abusive relationships usually have a 'magical consciousness' about such relationships, seeing them as inevitable as night and day. In such circumstances, consciousness-raising informal education about the possibility of living free of violence and abuse is threatening, exciting and alarming. Young men also may find the possibility of trying out less traditionally 'macho' approaches to relationships between young men and women both exciting and rather frightening. They too may feel vulnerable and in need of support as they try out different roles.

The conversation about violence for individual women who are involved in abusive relationships is fraught with difficulty. The violent power relationships, which are being challenged, create a barrier to any development through education. Non-threatening female spaces based on domestic activities traditionally associated with women–such as mother and toddler groups or cookery groups in which women may be free to participate–offer a space in which to explore alternatives. However, even when women are free to participate it may be some considerable time before they are able to talk about their experience. They may not want to admit the seriousness of their situation. Such denials can be challenged in safe and supportive spaces such as women's groups. The denial is often connected with disbelief: a woman's own disbelief that the violence is happening but also the disbelief (real or imagined) of family, of neighbours or of others. To be disbelieved in the context of such vulner-ability is to feel a little crazy. One of the purposes of informal education conversations in such contexts is to offer over and over again validation and belief, and to support men who wish to challenge other men about their abusive behaviour.

Another aspect of the conversation–and the internalised agendas associated with violence and abuse–is the consistent challenge to denigration. Much violence is rooted in a systematic practice of emotional undermining and attack, so the person on the receiving end of abuse comes to feel that it is at some level deserved.

Practice Example

'You are stupid.' 'You are incompetent.' 'You are ignorant.' 'You are an ugly unattractive bitch.' Statements such as these with their accompanying aggression and hurt need to be systematically challenged in conversation: 'You are resourceful', 'You are using your intelligence', and 'You are looking very pretty today'.

The eruption of anger or despair often involved in rights-based work needs to be carefully attended to. It may signal that the moment for further support and action has come: that a woman is ready to leave a violent relationship or to take further steps to engage in education.

The approach to work with both boys and girls within a project changes as the activities on offer change and the work becomes more conversational than most boys, certainly initially, expect.

The above exercise focuses on gender identities and the right to live free from violence. Throughout this book, informal learning is understood as offering support to young people as they develop a sense of identity and a sense of their capabilities, and as they learn about their rights. The meaning of identity is not however exhausted in the negotiation of rights and power.

Identity and a sense of self is also the basis from which we come to act in rela-tionship. Relationship is an equally significant theme of this book, and is particularly emphasised in later chapters. Developing the sense of 'ego' (the 'I' of 'I am') may be a fundamental requirement of the transition to adulthood. However, learning that **'I am because we are'** is also fundamental. This learning is as much concerned with love as it is with power. Learning to let go of 'ego', recognising the provisionality of all identities, may be as important to informal learning as the building up of ego and a sense of identity. Yet we may not abandon what we have never had. Identity-formation remains a key starting point for youth work engagement.

Identity as a basis for youth work practice matters because it is through identi-ties that power is struggled over, and it is through identities that people are positioned as 'normal' or 'deviant', 'us' or 'them'. The identity politics of the new social movements has had strong connections with the practice of informal educa-tion, particularly through consciousness-raising and activist research. It remains a major inspiration for youth and community work and for rights-based practice in the twenty-first century.

Key Terms

Identity as a significant basis for informal learning is inescapably complex and plural, and includes the meanings associated with a person's life narrative and the capacity to act from a sense of self.

Stereotypes are ways of constructing group identities, which render complex identities simple.

Double consciousness is produced by the interaction of both 'official' and subversive scripts and offers a basis for learning from identity.

The politics of identity as a politics of redistribution and recognition conceptualises the connection between identity and power.

Capability and rights are concepts that are universal in scope and provide a basis for anti-discriminatory practice.

Further Reading

Fraser, N. (1995) 'From redistribution to recognition. Dilemmas of justice in a post-socialist age', *New Left Review* 1(212), July–August. This text offers the basic account of the politics of identity, which underpins this chapter.

Rose, N. (1996) *Inventing Ourselves: Psychology, Power and Personhood*. New York and Cambridge: Cambridge University Press. This work explores the connection between subjectivity and power in democratic governance.

Sen, A. (1999) *Development as Freedom*. Oxford: Oxford University Press. Sen, with his colleague Martha Nussbaum, has developed a key philosophical basis for linking development, agency and rights.

Young, I. M. (2000) *Inclusion and Democracy*. Oxford: Oxford University Press. This extends and reframes Fraser's account in discussion of social difference as a political resource.

4

Social Inclusion and Exclusion: Challenging the 'NEET' Discourse

- Youth workers need to be able to recognise and analyse social policy discourses that direct and shape their work.
- Discourses of social inclusion and exclusion focus on social integration and the promotion of an image of society based on hard-working families.
- Where social integration fails, the existence of a 'moral underclass' discourse enables individual young people to be found morally culpable for their position and condemned rather than understood.
- Critical analysis offers alternative ways of seeing the possibilities for young people and for society as a whole. Valuable alternative traditions of practice to those focused on employability or on individual moral reform are the sources of examples of practice in this book.

'Start where you are.' 'Start where young people are at.' But what does it mean to identify a starting point?

All starting points are contestable. Why start here? Why not over there? And all conversation, even the most mundane and everyday, perhaps especially the most mundane and everyday, is full of contradictions and tensions. Youth workers need to be able to analyse such tensions and contradictions. Through this process the generative themes which form the conversational repertoire are identified.

Everyday 'common sense' is created from the traces of many ideological and belief systems, from religion and from science (Gramsci, 1971). The way we talk and make sense of the world in an everyday way is full of half-formed ideas whose sources are forgotten, including sayings and proverbs which usually offer several different muddled and contradictory ways of making sense of the world. 'It never rains but it pours.' 'Every cloud has a silver lining.' Such analysis of everyday talk enables us to understand the complex ways in which our own ideas and starting points are formed. The work of critical informal educators is concerned with the development of more coherent, more truthful and less fragmentary and contradictory views of the world. As well as analysing everyday talk contemporary discourse analysis also engages in the analysis of powerful discourses and the 'subject positions' they offer. 'Subject positions' are created by terms such as 'patient', 'young offender', 'NEET' (meaning 'Not in Education, Employment or Training') and 'service user'. They create ways in which young people and professionals are brought into relationship with one another. Critical analysis encourages the development of counter-discourses, which make a different sense of the world from the sense offered by dominant or 'official' discourses or scripts (Scott, 1990).

Policy discourse about young people and about poor communities in need of regeneration has shaped professional identities and job descriptions. Social policy is research-based to varying degrees (Coles, 2005). There is dispute as to the extent of 'evidence-based policy making' and a lively debate about attempts to mirror medical and health-based research, with the use of randomised controlled trials (Oakley, 2004–5; Spandler and Warner, 2007). Policy discourses are linked directly with funding, job descriptions, targets and the measurement of outcomes. Targets and outcomes both prescribe job descriptions and circumscribe and limit practice. Staff with the ability to subject these aspects of their work to analysis are able to see what is being closed down and what is being opened up as a result of such policy frameworks.

The rest of this chapter offers a worked example of what is involved in the critical analysis of social policy discourses of inclusion and exclusion.

Discourses of inclusion and exclusion

Discourses of inclusion/exclusion are found not just in policy documents but also in the mass media and in the everyday talk of professionals in the workplace. The discourse of inclusion/exclusion builds on previous discourses–such as 'equal opportunities' discourses–and is being challenged by new constructions, such as those surrounding cohesion and security. Every discourse closes down some conversations and opens up others. Critical analysis aims to make clear how such rhetoric operates. Young people themselves may well offer the best clues to the operation of powerful policy agendas by a mute resistance to taking part in conversations based on them, even on relatively 'safe' and uncontroversial topics such as 'healthy eating' (Spence and Devanney, 2007).

Analysis creates space for new directions in conversation and for new experiences. People marginalised or objectified in policy discourses can recognise themselves as subjects and agents in their own lives. Critical informal education conversations can then start where people are and ask questions about it, not leave them there. It moves them from point (a), their starting point, to a point beyond (a) (Davies, 2005).

Social integrationist discourse and moral underclass discourse (Levitas, 2004) are both strongly present in youth policy. They provide the framework in which funds are allocated for posts and job descriptions written. Both offer a clear role to educators.

In *a social integrationist discourse*, youth and community workers are understood as bridge-builders and creators of social capital (Field, 2003). The aim of social integration is to prevent the breakdown of the social whole and to include people who might be 'outsiders'. This is often conceptualised in terms of including people into the dominant ethos of the nation on already existing terms: so the image of a democratic society committed to certain freedoms and to an ethos of 'hard-working families' sets the terms for inclusion and integration.

In *a moral underclass discourse*, the role of the youth and community worker is to bring about either the moral reform or the control of pathologically troubled individuals and families. Certain groups of people are seen as (by nature or upbringing) incapable of joining the mainstream of society and as undermining its morality. They are considered a 'moral underclass' or residuum, threatening the rest of us. Both social integrationist and moral underclass discourses tend to silence issues of inequality in the distribution of resources and power.

The first step of critical analysis is to recognise what particular discourses have to say about the people with whom the informal educator is working, and what they tend to silence or render invisible.

Rhetorical figures: how young people are seen in policy discourse

One way of doing this is to pay attention to the rhetorical figures that come to symbolise and make concrete the issues of inclusion/exclusion. Within the flow of meaning, key rhetorical figures emerge. Such figures often hold a concentration of meaning concerning who and what is inside and who and what is outside. These 'cuts' in the flow of meaning produce as well as describe identities, creating a specific cultural construction of 'them' and 'us', a separation which is always violent, and which has material effects (Hall, 1990).

The production of such rhetorical figures and their amplification through the signification spirals of moral panics is a process which has been widely documented since the term was first coined by sociologist Stan Cohen in *Folk Devils and Moral Panics* (1972). Youth workers need to recognise such processes as they occur. In each generation, young men and young women are likely to be caught up in these spirals of escalating reporting and policy response. They find themselves belonging to groups in which they are not only doing their own growing up but also carrying a set of burdens and projections for the whole society. The rhetorical figures are sometimes *'demons'* (as in Cohen's classic account of mods and rockers) but not always. They are also quite commonly represented as *victims* of disease and/or of social pathology, as is often the case with victims of drug-related deaths or of bullying.

These rhetorical figures point to the themes of a wider social crisis. Resolution of the crisis through scapegoating is a common outcome of 'moral panic': the control or even expulsion of those represented by the rhetorical figure. Such scapegoating has frequently been a convenient and powerful response to social problems. Analysis of the rhetoric suggests something about the fears and choices facing the society, taking the 'burden of representation' away from young people and opening the way to a more generous imagination of the social whole.

Discussion Point

As long ago as 1986, Phil Cohen suggested that the task of analysis in youth studies was to focus attention on the 'multiply divided subject in the multiply divided whole' (Cohen, 1997: 223). One of the functions of these rhetorical figures is to divert such attention from, for example, social divisions and power relations of class, gender or post-colonial culture and from the internal division which they constitute in the multiply divided subjects of the culture. They produce a sense of a unified 'us' (who are respectable, not anti-social; who are sexually chaste, not promiscuous; who are English, not Asian; Christian, not Muslim) and also of 'them'.

Which young people are the focus of attention as you read this book? What are they leading attention away from today?

Three such figures are considered here: the ASBO; the 'Asian' youth; and the pregnant teenager.

ASBO

The Anti-Social Behaviour Order (ASBO) was introduced in 1999 following the Crime and Disorder Act of 1998. By spring 2005, out of 3,069 applications for ASBOs to civil magistrates' courts, only 42 had been refused. These orders rest on a bewilderingly vague definition of anti-social behaviour: 'behaviour which has caused (or is likely to cause) harassment, alarm or distress to others.' By 2005, 46 per cent of the orders had been on juveniles and some 50 young people were in custody for breaching an ASBO. Breach of ASBO was claimed by some commentators to be the most significant cause of the rise in custodial sentences for young people in this period (Thomas, 2005).

ASBOs work through mobilisation of local views as to what is anti-social. This provides an important mechanism for the channelling of fears and anxieties via the local press and other local news reporting. When the Home Affairs Committee discussed ASBOs in 2005 it concluded that the lack of definition was a positive factor in the success of the ASBO. They concluded that

- definitions worked well from an enforcement point of view and no significant practical problems appear to have been encountered;
- exhaustive lists of behaviour considered anti-social by central government would be unworkable and anomalous;
- anti-social behaviour is inherently a local problem and should be defined at local level.

This has not limited the national reporting of cases and the use of glossy flyers 'naming and shaming' the recipients of ASBOs, as reporting restrictions which apply to young people charged with criminal offences do not apply to civil magistrates' courts. All of this happened during a period in which governments might have benefited from a steep decline in the crime rate, a well-established international trend. Between 1995 and 1999, there had been a 23 per cent fall in the crime rate, and this was not restricted to property crimes: there had been a 20 per cent decline in violent crime over the same period. Only homicide continued in its progress, rising 1 per cent rise a year: a serious crime which has very specific causes. Yet the same period in which social exclusion/inclusion strategies were emphasised saw a massive increase in the prison population. The number of children in custody has increased by more than 50 per cent since 1992 and the length of time spent in custody has doubled, at the same time as the use of community-based sanctions has increased (NAPO, 2005; LGA, 2006).

Like the 'hoodie', the 'ASBO' (the word moves from the order to the person) is a rhetorical figure which speaks much of the fears in particular communities. Fear is easily intensified through media amplification, leading to new political interventions, such as the now acceptable short-cutting of judicial procedures and consequent loss of civil liberties for those suspected of 'breaches of security' and terrorism (Thomas, 2007).

Asian youth/Muslim youth

Many current representations of 'Asian youth' signify 'difference', the 'outsider within'. This discourse powerfully shapes perception both by politicians and by the public as a whole. When Brazilian Jean de Menezes was tragically shot dead by police at Stockwell tube station following the July bombings in London in 2005, many eyewitnesses reported that they saw 'someone Asian' being shot.

Even prior to the bombings in London, Asian youth were already seen as embodying difference and otherness, whether in the figure of the woman in the hijab or the figure of the young man from a 'Northern town' whose family has migrated from a Pakistani or Bangladeshi village community. Segregated ghettos, it was suggested, had developed in towns such as Bradford, Oldham and Burnley. These communities signified 'failure to integrate' in the public imagination. Segregation was a key theme of government reports (Cantle, 2001; Denham, 2002). Media debate focused on issues of language acquisition and British cultural identity. From these discussions citizenship classes and citizenship ceremonies for those acquiring citizenship emerged, although the communities where cohesion was found to be lacking had been established for forty years.

The Cantle Report emphasised the possibility of youth workers' involvement in the creation of social capital, citizenship and a democratic voice, against a background of economic decline, and social and cultural isolation (Thomas, 2003). Racist abuse sparked the disturbances of 2001, yet in this context Cantle turned the focus of policy attention away from institutional racism, which had been emerging as a focus of policy, on to young men who were seen as 'disaffected', perceived as 'outsiders within'. The rhetorical figure of the Asian youth condenses many fears of the 'unintegrated and uninvited outsider'. These fears have circulated with such power that, in August 2006, students travelling home to Manchester were asked to leave a flight on which they were booked, as other passengers suspected them of being terrorists. They were guilty only of the charge of travelling by air while looking Asian.

Teenage mothers

In 1999, the UK had the highest rate of teenage pregnancies in Europe: twice as high as Germany, three times as high as France, and six times that of the Netherlands. The Social Exclusion Unit set a target of achieving a 50 per cent reduction in the rate of teenage conceptions by 2010, but it was announced in 2006 that that this target would not be achieved and that little progress had been made. 'Britain's youngest mother' is a regular feature (though a very unpopular figure) in the tabloid press. Discourses surrounding the teenage mother in the drive against social exclusion were prefigured historically by Conservative Government's attention to the impact of support to such mothers on the public purse. Some Conservatives were also concerned about the ways in which traditional morality is undermined by support for 'unmarried mothers'. Policy discussion of teenage mothers in the context of social exclusion (Social Exclusion Unit, 1999; DOH, 2004) continued this largely negative emphasis, but this time with an apparent stress on the risks to the well-being of the young women, rather than the risks to the state. The risks have been reported as follows:

- Poverty is a key risk factor. Young women from the lowest social class are ten times more likely to become teenage mothers than young women from the highest social class.
- Children in care or leaving care are more likely to become teenage parents.
- Daughters of teenage mothers are more likely to become teenage mothers themselves.
- Low educational achievement is shown to be a risk factor, along with truancy and social exclusion.
- An association between sexual abuse in childhood and teenage pregnancy has been found. (42nd Street, 2005)

Many of these could be seen as the effects of poverty rather than the effects of pregnancy. The emphasis on the negative effects on the well-being of young women apparently brought about by pregnancy leads to a view of young women as 'vulnerable victims'. The overall negativity of the discourse surrounding teenage pregnancy has its all too predictable effects.

Practice Example

'No-one has said to me that I'm not a good mother but teenage mothers get put down so much that maybe when you've heard it so much you kind of start believing it's true.' (Nadia, 18) (42nd Street, *Not Exactly Congratulations*, 2005)

How would your practice respond to Nadia?

Analysing the rhetoric

'Hoodies' and 'ASBOs' have been presented as 'feral youth' occupying the borderlands between the human/animal, and potentially out of control. The teenage pregnancy rate is also 'out of control' and perhaps the sexuality which underlies it is 'out of control' too, uncivilised and excessive. Projected on to the terrifying figure of the Asian youth is an apparently uncontrollable fear, arising from a denial of global connectedness, particularly the consequences of colonialism and then war.

This need to exert control and containment repeats one of the well-established discourses about adolescence in which the progress from child/adult is thought of as progress from uncivilised to civilised, from the primitive to the rational. In this account, adolescence is a time when the primitive (sexual) urges of nature meet culture (in the form of institutions of transition and of social integration). As Phil Cohen put it:

> It is interesting that this characterisation of adolescents as a hybrid species, half-animal, half-human corresponds almost exactly to the position assigned to colonial populations and the domestic working classes in the discourses of liberal imperialism. (Cohen, 1997: 184)

Rhetorical figures serve to carry a shift from 'structural' understandings of the causes of social exclusion to explanations which focus on the (usually deficient) 'agency', that is the behaviours and choices, of individual young people (Colley and Hodkinson, 2001). Much research into exclusion makes a fundamental link with poverty, with the structure of the labour market and the low-pay/no-pay spiral. The power of individuals to escape poverty and exclusion through social mobility has lessened and the gap between the poorest sections of society and the rest has not diminished and in fact has increased (JRF, 2006). However, the policy discourses and education-based interventions, including youth work interventions, which focus individualistically on young people's capacity to bring about significant changes in their lives by 'pulling themselves up by their own boot-straps' distracts professionals from such realities. It locates the experience of exclusion in the agency, or rather the lack of agency, of individuals who experience it, who are told 'You can do it if you really want .....'

The 'agency' of the 'socially excluded' is usually perceived as quite limited. In contrast with 'can do' young people and 'active citizens' who are considered 'included', the rhetorical figures condense into the one symbolic figure of the 'NEET'. This acronym, which is in common use to refer to young people, characterises them as having a problem about being fully autonomous, self-governing and self-directed. Interventions in their lives are based on a calculation of 'risk': either the risk they pose (usually boys) or the risk they are at (usually girls). Unlike their 'included' counterparts who are (allegedly) planning their life paths from a very young age, taking control of their destinies, young people who are excluded are perceived as unable to be the subjects of their own lives and become instead the objects of policy interventions designed to transform these risky characters into 'hard-working families.'

The purpose of social policy: social integration through hard work

What civilises? What disciplines? Work, above all, and so policy initiatives strive, in the language of the Connexions strategy, to turn 'NEETs' into 'EETs'. First teenage pregnancy units, then Youth Offending Teams, then Drugs Action Teams developed a strategy focusing on education, employment and training, encouraging employability and insisting that the jobs on offer are taken.

Constructions of an integrated society also suggest a preference for a model of relationship and family life consisting of regulated co-habiting (heterosexual) couples forming stable and healthy two-parent families. Through good parenting, then, many social issues may be tackled. Both sexual health initiatives and parenting initiatives too readily come to focus on issues such as sexually transmitted diseases or on ill health caused by obesity. They involve an implicit model of the family as a source of moral education, in particular an education in restraint both sexual and gastronomic. Furthermore, the rhetoric of a society constructed in a common language and culture (and perhaps out of nostalgia for a common 'Church of England' type religion) contains an implicit image of the 'inside' with which 'outsiders' are invited to integrate: a multicultural society based on 'British' values of freedom, hard work, decency and fair play, suggesting that these values, which are commonly thought to be universal, are connected to a particular nationality, and that their absence in some people may be due to their 'foreignness'.

All these discourses provoke resistance as well as compliance. Teenagers continue to seem disinclined, in the face of the health agendas of the 'corporate parent', to use contraception or practise safe sex, and they even fail systematically to eat five portions of fruit and vegetables a day. In response to calls for integration, the adoption of Islamic codes of dress and appearance as a way of marking difference grows stronger in the face of community cohesion strategies which emphasise 'finding the common ground'. Border skirmishes–as these resistances are sometimes called–suggest the need for ever greater vigilance and ever increasing control. When 'social integration' fails, what is left is taken as evidence that the families and children who are excluded form a 'moral underclass' who cannot be developed and must simply be controlled. All the discourses surrounding social exclusion/inclusion have some apparatus of control associated with them. Still, the resistance to containment and control and the difficulties that inclusion strategies face may suggest something about alternative and new ways of imagining the whole.

When integration fails ...

One of the key mechanisms of moral underclass discourse is the publicising of shameful figures and shameful events associated with them, and the production of explanations for them which reframe issues of power and politics as moral issues and/or as issues of social pathology. When conflict emerges, as it does again and again, it is most commonly figured not as arising from fractures within society, but as a war against society. Policy discourse then, in a signification spiral, adopts a military tone–'the war on drugs', 'the war on terror'–and we hear talk of activities occurring 'beneath the radar'. One consequence of the need for control as a back-up strategy when 'improving employability' fails is that staff working on 'social inclusion' projects have come to accept a high level of surveillance and security in the workplace. CCTV is universal and some schools now employ security guards on a regular basis. The 'client' appears routinely to be perceived as a violent individual and projects, as well as doctors' surgeries, A & E departments and public therapy clinics, are plastered with notices to clients telling them that violent and abusive behaviour is not acceptable. Indeed, low level aggression and pressure are anticipated as an aspect of much social interaction. Rather than being understood as systemic, this is seen both as an individual client's problem (leading either to medical intervention or to criminalisation) and as something to be contained by the right kind of professional approach. NEETs are relentlessly being encouraged to become EETs through such initiatives as school exclusion projects, accreditation of informal learning, community computing and many more.

The return of the repressed: desires for satisfying work, satisfying relationships, global connectedness

In the practices of containment so much that is possible has been avoided.

The problem of low pay/low skill employment

There is little discussion of the nature of some young people's realistic expectations of education, training and a working life and the kinds of jobs that may be available to them. If the goal is reduction of extreme poverty, we know that what needs reforming is not the individual worker but the labour market itself and the spread of low-wage unstable work (Fahmy, 2005). The low-paid are more likely than the highly paid to become unemployed in the next year. They are also more likely to be low-paid on returning to work. Seventy per cent of the low-paid care sector is female. Casual labour in the service sector characterises the part-time employment of many young people. There are one million fewer young workers working full time in the labour market in the UK than there were in 1971. This is partially explained by population but largely by the fact that so many now remain in education and training and then work part time. The minimum wage for 16-year-olds, introduced at £3 an hour and at £4.10 for 17–22-year-olds institutionalises both age discrimination and the expectation of dependency. This suggests that early experiences of working life may not be ones that lead to the independence and autonomy so beloved of the proponents of 'hard-working families'. Rather, 'dependency' is transferred from the state to families or else to illegal means of livelihood.

Care and relationships

There is little room for discussion of alternative, more creative and fulfilling uses of time than those provided by paid employment; little contemplation of the spaces of leisure or of care and relationships. The lack of a central image of a society which prioritises care and relationship above paid work is particularly disastrous for women for whom child care arrangements, arrangements for the care of elders and negotiation of adult relationships with partners and ex-partners so often take priority over commitment to paid work. Low-paid work characteristically demands long hours in stressful conditions, which diminishes the time available to nurture and supervise children, or to support others in times of need.

The focus on a moralised set of family relationships forecloses discussion of many issues concerning the place of choice and reproductive rights in the teenage years. The capability of young people in the UK (compared with their European counterparts) to make positive use of information about contraception and abortion, and to negotiate their heterosexual (or indeed homosexual) relationships in ways that enable them to lead happy and fulfilled lives seems limited. The reality of many adult family relationships is now a long way from the traditional image of the nuclear family, but there is little to suggest that the worst fears of either the Conservative right or the critics of the left who see a frighteningly atomised and individualised future are being borne out. Rather, women in particular are paying attention to nurturing a network of relationships, in which the support needs of their children takes priority. It is realities such as these which are repressed in the rhetorical figures at work in social inclusion discourses.

Don't talk about the war

'Social inclusion' is a domestic policy, whilst 'war' is a part of foreign policy. However, to deny the impact of foreign policies on domestic agendas has become impossible in an age of globalisation. At the time of writing, the international context of war and terror is one that is scarcely ever referred to in policies on social inclusion/exclusion. Yet the locals are connected globally, and local policies are constructed with an eye to anti-terrorist strategies at the same time as seeking to promote 'community cohesion'. Those who cannot speak English are suspect. Yet youth and community work projects often take place in communities in which the desire to find a different kind of global connectedness from that characterised by war is extremely strong. When they take place in the poorest communities, they are also taking place in areas from which recruits to the armed forces are most likely to be drawn.

Resources for practitioners: hidden from history?

In many voluntary sector organisations, with their roots in collectives and co-operatives, there is an important history of commitment to fair treatment of staff, relatively flat hierarchies in the workplace, co-operative working practices and attention to work–life balance. It is a very hard-pressed tradition.

A second important resource from the history of informal learning is the emphasis on play, culture and creativity. Most recently this was to be found in the adventure playground movement, in many aspects of outdoor and wilderness education, and in projects which draw on the visual arts (photography and community arts based activity), on drama workshops and on music, and now on the new digital media, as ways of living through and working through what's interesting and what matters to young people. Such arts-based work allows the exploration of alternative framings and ways of making sense of experience. It enables different ways of imagining the future to those offered by the 'employability' discourses associated with social inclusion strategies. In particular, it can nurture emotion and imagination as critical resources for creating 'greater expectations' among young people.

Thirdly, there is a tradition of sexuality and sex education, particularly associated with feminist initiatives, which emphasises self-worth, pleasure and negotiation, as well as access to and information about contraception and abortion. The focus is on education and enjoyment, and on the importance of 'informed consent' so that young men and women can make choices about their lives rather than feel 'fated' by the messages that surround them. For many young women living in poverty, motherhood is a more positive option than low-paid work. This need not exclude a return to education as a basis for self-development rather than merely 'employability'.

Fourthly, traditions of political education, now being articulated as global education, enable the exploration of issues of war and peace. The organisation of international exchanges and involvement in 'welcome' projects for new migrants, including asylum seekers from the global war zones, are essential aspects of this practice.

Informal groupwork with self-selected peer groups and culturally specific and inter-cultural work of a variety of kinds are central informal education strategies. This takes the focus away from *reform* of the individual (although it can continue that theme into the 'reform of group cultures') to the *development* of the individual within a group: an educational focus. Groupwork has long been valued as a democratic method, as contributing to the development of civil society, and to the critique of pathologising discourses in social policy. It can create a basis for mutual support and self-help in an increasingly individualised society, and is frequently cited as contributing to the development of social capital.

All these traditions can engage in critical partnership with work undertaken as a result of social inclusion/exclusion discourses, because they enable alternative and frequently repressed aspects of social existence to be explored, while also delivering the much sought after 'outcomes' of the social integration discourse. These alternative models of practice, often drawn from urban contexts, form the basis for the discussions of good practice in the rest of this book. It is important to recognise that all critical practice with young people starts by being implicated in the social policy discourses which surround young people. There is no alternative but to struggle with the discourses in order to recognise their impact, value the resources they offer but also, where necessary, to devise ways and means of countering their negative constructions of young people and their potential.

Key Terms

Moral panics arise as a means of marking the boundaries of social and moral order. As representations of escalating public disorder, they are of real importance both to generations of young people, whose lives become publicly visible and remembered through them, and to youth workers who need to help them make sense of them.

Social integration is a durable policy discourse which develops in response to the fragmenting tendencies of the free market and emphasises 'belonging', especially when it is achieved through work and making a contribution to society.

Moral underclass refers to a construction in policy discourse in which communities and families who have experienced worklessness, poverty and sometimes criminalisation for decades are seen as deficient either genetically or in character and morality.

Further Reading

Jeffs, T. and Smith, M.K. (2006) 'Where is Youth Matters taking us?' *Youth and Policy*, 91: 23–40. This text offers a good example of a consistent theme in Jeffs and Smith's work, on the containment and control of young people proposed in much UK social policy.

Levitas, R. (2004) *The Inclusive Society? Social Exclusion and New Labour*. Basingstoke: Palgrave Macmillan. This text offers an introduction to the analysis of social policy which underpins this chapter.

Thompson, K. (1998) *Moral Panics*. London and New York: Routledge. This text offers a clear and accessible account of the sociological analysis of moral panics, starting from the mods and rockers.

5

Personal Agendas: Reflective Practice in the Context of Diversity

- The personal voice and presence of the informal educator in relationship and conversation with young people is a major resource of practice. This demands a commitment to reflective practice.
- Reflective practice must take seriously the existence of power-charged diversity in working relationships.
- A case study of reflective practice in the context of diversity is developed using the Johari window.
- Methods of reflective practice, including giving and receiving feedback and the use of practice journals, are discussed.

Practitioners bring their own personal agendas into practice, their own starting points, prejudices and assumptions. The explicit professional agenda of youth and community work is the flourishing and development of young people and of their communities. The core purpose of youth work is 'the personal and social development of young people through informal education' (Merton et al., 2004). Alongside this professional agenda, everyone also has personal passions, preoccupations and prejudices which form a personal agenda. The extent to which these agendas are visible both to practitioners and to the people with whom they work needs to be a matter for regular reflection. In particular, our ability to recognise and take steps to counter prejudice in ourselves, or to recognise limitations in our knowledge and understanding, is vital. 'Reflective practice must take seriously the context of "power-charged diversity"' (Haraway, 1991b; Palmer, 2002). The educators must be educated.

Motivations for informal education

Some of the most powerful motivations for involvement in youth and community work occur at a non-rational level. Informal education engages our passions and emotions as well as our thoughts. Such motivations may remain hidden from the practitioner for a considerable time.

For example, the question of which groups of young people we are drawn to work with and why is interesting. The answers are not always immediately obvious. Why do some practitioners find themselves drawn to particular so-called 'hard to reach' groups, such as young offenders or young people suffering mental health difficulties? Why do some women and some men enjoy working on issues of gender with women-only groups or men-only groups while others prefer to work in mixed groups of men and women? These questions of liking and preference are not simple or entirely rational. However, they can and ought to be made explicit and explored. In undertaking such reflective practice, the committed practitioner begins to disentangle their own motivation and agendas for engaging in the work from those of the young people, who do after all have their own agendas. Reflective practice is well supported by regular supervision, which is now established as an essential support to the work of therapists and counsellors. It should be regarded as equally essential to those working in informal education projects with young people (Hawkins and Shohet, 2003).

It is often suggested that to be professional means to be objective and neutral with respect to the agendas of young people, for example the question of what they have reason to value. Others argue that this stance leads to a powerful denial of personal investment in professional identities. The consequence of such denial is that the impact of powerful personal investments on others remains closed to scrutiny. Youth and community workers need to be as aware as they can be of their own perspectives and motivations if their work with young people is to be freed to support the young person's own decision-making and flourishing. Paradoxically, the recognition of personal agendas on the part of practitioners is the best method of avoiding imposing them on young people. It is of course possible, while being completely unethical, deliberately to operate with a covert agenda: seeking converts to a particular faith or political cause for example. The method of 'reflective practice' discussed in this chapter offers a professional framework which challenges covert working.

'Conscious use of self in relation to others' connects the professional identity of the youth and community worker with their personal identity, and enables them to become resourceful in relation to the identity struggles of the young people they are working with. Reflective practice needs to be developed in ways which address issues of identity, power and conflict.

The 'conscious use of self in relation to others'

The 'Johari window' is a commonly used starting point for the exploration of self. Drawing on psychodynamic models which understand the self as divided and formed in both conscious and unconscious ways, the four areas of the Johari window offer a starting point for reflective practice. They provide a method for exploring prejudices or assumptions based on lack of knowledge. They also provide a means for challenging the denial of the importance of 'difference' and 'power'.

The Johari window

Quadrant I. The area of free activity or public area, refers to behaviour and motivation known to self and to others. This will include the open professional definitions of the work in which the youth and community worker is engaged

Quadrant II. The blind area: here others can see things in ourselves of which we are unaware. This can include both strengths and weaknesses. It is the place in which both positive and constructively critical feedback can be hard to receive. The extent of our personal lack of self-awareness of course shifts as a result of feedback, and changes over time, and in new situations and contexts. No one is ever fully self-aware.

Quadrant III. The avoided or hidden areas, represents things we know but do not reveal to others (e.g. a hidden agenda, or matters about which we have sensitive feelings). This may well include personal matters which might be judged harshly by others such as personal histories of ill health or of mental health difficulties, personal knowledge of drug cultures, prejudices or behaviours about which we have been confronted in the past and which reflect badly on us.

Quadrant IV. Areas of unknown activity, in which neither the individual nor others are aware of certain behaviours or motives. Yet we can assume their existence through experience because of the situations in which it eventually becomes apparent that some previously unknown and unrecognised behaviours and motives were influencing our relationship all along. These are often not easily available to our consciousness, or there is a block in our understanding of them.

The four quadrants draw attention to material that is open to self and to others, available for public discussion and conversation; material that is available to self and not to others about which we choose to remain private yet recognise as influencing us; material that is available to others and not to self, our 'blind spots'; and lastly, and arguably most powerfully, material that is available neither to self nor to others but which is operating unconsciously and present non-verbally through jokes, slips of the tongue and other non-conscious levels of communication. One of the most complex features of the use of the Johari window for giving and receiving critical feedback is in relation to a *shared unawareness* in which giver and receiver are complicit. It is possible to use systematic attention to feelings of uncertainty or sensitivity to begin to probe and explore such areas, as the following hypothetical case study is designed to show.

The Johari window in the context of diversity: a case study

A diverse team of women workers is proposing to develop work with Black young men. The broad aims of the work include the opening up of opportunities for further education to Black young men, but the specific project details and 'outcomes' are relatively open. Using the Johari window could open up discussion of the impact of diversity in the following ways.

The first quadrant: Open and free activity.
The language of the professional

In professional policy language, there are commonly used racialised and politicised references to groups. The term 'Black and Minority Ethnic Communities' is commonly shortened to 'BME' in professional talk. The term 'diverse' is also used euphemistically to refer to the same groups. Each of these terms points to the existence of power struggles in which issues of 'race' discrimination have been made visible and yet not fully engaged with.

Racial discrimination is discrimination based on skin colour or other commonly designated 'racial' attributes. The term 'race' is placed in inverted commas to show that it is a social construction arising from racism, not a biological category. 'One race, the human race.'

Probing the exact understanding of the term 'Black', when it is used as part of the term 'BME' is essential. It was originally a political marker claimed by communities of African heritage who experienced racial discrimination on the basis of skin colour. In the often-used pairing, 'Black and Asian' it may seem that some communities are referred to by skin colour and others by culture. Similarly the term 'Asian' needs investigation. If 'Asian' designates an 'ethnicity', in what sense is it a minority ethnicity? To whom do the people designated 'ethnic minorities' become visible as 'minorities'? If particular people are designated as 'diverse', who are the people who are not 'diverse', who are just 'themselves'? The invisibility of 'Whiteness' in policy documents (other than in the census and therefore in the sampling categories of research projects designed to investigate some aspect of 'diversity') supports its dominance. 'Whiteness' occupies the invisible norm. 'Others' who are from Black and minority ethnic groups are addressed as 'special interest' groups, potentially seen as 'lacking' and pathological, rather than structurally disadvantaged.

Even if a team of educators wishes to situate themselves as neutral professionals, they cannot in fact escape being positioned by a racialising and politicising discourse (Delgado, 2001). As professionals, members of the team recognise one another as such. But the term 'Black professional' has come into existence because of an exclusion operating in the category of 'professional'. The assumption has been that a professional is 'white' unless otherwise stated. A member of this team of women workers who is positioned as 'Black' may experience her professionalism as being questioned by those she works with in a different way from her white colleagues.

The space of professional discussion is proposed as a space of open and free discussion. A major task is to extend this space of open communication and to transform its terms, whether in staff teams or with young people. In this case, staff have taken on a particular role in relation to widening participation, are being paid for what they are doing, and are reasonably expected to undertake their work with honesty, reliability and in a spirit of fairness. This code of ethics is open and visible. The professional space is concerned with access to higher and further education. There is a body of resources in the form of space, time, money and learning opportunities. There is power: the power of the gatekeeper to open and close doors of opportunity. And in consequence there are opportunities to engage in inter-professional settings in order to challenge discourses which render Black colleagues invisible and likely to be perceived as 'unprofessional'.

The second quadrant: The blind area. Making 'whiteness' visible

Whilst the problem of 'class' in education is well recognised, especially in relationships between schools and some predominantly working-class communities, the fact and meaning of 'colour' has been much less often discussed professionally. Particularly for those team members whose 'colour' is not a common reference point, and who are participating in the privileged invisibility of 'whiteness', 'colour' may appear insignificant. They may never have used racialised language to describe themselves, and may not even be aware that the sense of 'colour' and the ascribing of meanings to 'colour' happens 'all ways', not just in relation to Blackness. However, even if they do not see themselves as 'white', they are likely to be perceived as such by the young men they are proposing to work with, who in turn are quite accustomed to seeing themselves and to being seen by others in terms of 'race' based on appraisals of skin tone.

Being 'inside our own skins', it is not easy to gain a sense of how we might be seen by others, although it will be more obvious to people who have been subject to racism. In this project, attention to 'masculinity' is also involved. Seeing ourselves as others see us also involves seeing across the 'difference' and potential attractions and hostilities of gender. Both 'whiteness' and 'masculinity' have historically been associated with dominance, and so, in this context, each group–the team of women workers and the young Black men who are to be involved in the outreach project–has been constructed, in dominant representations, as potentially threatening to the other. Being aware of the existence of these constructions means that we are in a better position to undermine and challenge them in our relationships. It also leads to an explicit recognition of the ways in which the Black women members of the team are positioned to act as *bridgers* who may enable the work to happen.

A significant shift can then be made away from notions of the 'neutral professional' and towards a more situated perspective. This enables a sense of the strengths and limitations from which not just individuals but the team is working. A team who can recognise the significance of the discourses surrounding 'race', femininity and masculinity as well as class can hear new things, which either open up or close down conversation and informal learning.

There may be a choice to downplay the significance of meanings and topics associated with 'race' and 'difference' and to find points of connection, such as shared interests and enthusiasms or shared investments in the life of a particular neighbourhood or city. Alternatively, the conversation can explicitly engage with issues of 'race' and racism in order to form an alliance in an anti-racist project of for example desegregation of provision, or positive affirmative action with the young men. What each of these strategies seeks explicitly to move away from is a position of 'whiteness' as natural and taken for granted superiority and the consequent positioning of non-whiteness as subordinate, marginal and excluded. In order to do this, it is necessary to see 'whiteness', to be prepared to see ourselves and our contexts as they appear to others, to denaturalise all that seems natural and normal. It is not only important to *see* 'whiteness'. It is important to *hear* and take in information about the consequences of 'whiteness' as a form of superiority. 'Being proud to be white' and 'Being proud to be Black' are not equivalents in a society that has historically privileged 'whiteness' and stigmatised 'Blackness'. Yet the need to have a sense of self-worth and a sense of identity in which we can feel some pride and belonging is an important one in all communities, however they have been 'coloured'.

The third quadrant: The avoided or hidden areas. Don't make assumptions

It is likely that the gender of a team of women workers is visible to all, yet it is wrong to assume that this automatically creates a set of shared meanings. The presence of a group of women is open to a number of conflicting interpretations, which are not immediately visible. Some women may see their womanhood as not very important. They see themselves first and foremost as individuals doing a job alongside men as equals. To others, being a woman seems a restriction, a source of frustration, and is accompanied by a sense of injustice and inequality. To still others, being a woman is first and foremost about being a mother. These are different repertoires in which an account of their gender can be given. The team of women practitioners might perhaps be a group of feminist or womanist practitioners, or women of faith, or all of these. As well as the potential different ideological and philosophical interpretations of gender that might be present, there is likely to be a range of personal experiences that are not necessarily immediately visible. Some of them are part of African-Caribbean heritage families. Such themes are all part of potentially hidden agendas and tacit knowledges, but when made explicit they offer potential sources of knowledge and information for the practice of informal education and potential bridges into conversation.

One of the most difficult hidden or avoided areas is that of uncovering or exploring prejudice. The consequence of living in a world that has been structured historically by racism and sexism and class is the existence of an enormous repertoire of prejudices and stereotypes. As committed practitioners, we despise such prejudices and regard ourselves as liberals and thus may find it very hard to acknowledge the part that such prejudices have played in our own formation. Yet there is no one who has been untouched by prejudices about 'others' and it is important that this is acknowledged, not in order to produce 'confessions of guilt', but to free the space for educational activity.

Becoming aware of how our own cultural background, including the unfounded assumptions and prejudices, as well as the resources, of that background, influences our practice is an essential. The tendency to assume non-prejudice rather than to examine and attempt to deconstruct prejudice is powerful in professional groups, who are all too ready to seek to challenge prejudice among the groups of young people with whom they are working. This is a major block to good practice. If we seek to tackle prejudice in informal conversations with young people, we must first of all address prejudice in ourselves. We need to recognise the roots of prejudice in lack of knowledge, but also in fear, and in prevailing ideologies which support division. It may be possible to excavate the well-denied experience of prejudice among professionals by asking questions such as 'Who would it have been most difficult for you to take home as a potential partner?' 'What was the prevailing view of this (frequently stereotyped) group in the family you grew up in?' 'Name ten stereotypes that you are aware of about the groups you are working with.' Being aware of the capacities of such prejudices to continue to influence us even when we wish to disown them is a significant contribution to neutralising their power.

The fourth quadrant: Unknown activity … Only joking!

Finally, reflective practice can seek to engage with powerful material on the edge of consciousness, not available to self or to others at the level of consciousness but making itself felt through lapses in communication, through silences, jokes, slips of the tongue, non-verbal communication, in metaphors and figures of speech and even in dreams. This is the landscape of emotion, in particular of desire and repulsion, attraction and disgust, anxiety and fear, passion and commitment, guilt and shame, anger and joy, attachment and rejection. Such feelings are all too rarely spoken about. Practitioners need to ask themselves questions such as 'How are you feeling about what is happening here?' It is particularly important, in the context of safe anti-oppressive practice, to be alert to feelings of isolation, feelings of being overwhelmed or bombarded and feelings of being threatened. Such feelings should signal the need to seek out support or 'time out' from the pressures of practice.

Informal education as a practice always engages the emotions. Practitioners must be able to recognise and name emotional work as part of professional practice. Intuitions, hunches, feelings that have yet to be given a name are highly significant. Informal education practice is not therapy, in that it does not seek to work primarily with unconscious material. It is however essential to recognise the power and presence of such material. Why do some situations make us passionate while others, objectively equally important, leave us cold? What do we find exciting and what frustrating about the work we are undertaking? What makes us feel uncomfortable, even ashamed?

In the example we have been investigating here–a diverse team of women workers setting out to undertake a project of outreach work with young Black men– emotions of attraction, empathy, care, and pride as well as, potentially, fear and guilt might all be anticipated. If such feelings are named, they can be recognised and made to work for the project.

It may be recognised that some feelings are so powerful as to make the piece of work a non-starter. Guilt in particular has been noted and analysed as a significant block in attempting to create inter-cultural or inter-'racial' communication. Guilt quite often paralyses action as it focuses emotional attention on the guilty person. It leads one to become self-absorbed. In this it differs from another related emotion, shame at injustice, which, it is argued, propels those who experience it towards acts of justice and restitution. A further danger lies in the potential for the dynamic of the roles of persecutor/victim/ rescuer to become the key dynamic. This version of 'solidarity' has been a common one in the past, particularly in charitable work. It has been seen as itself a pattern of cultural racism, reinforcing the superiority of 'whiteness' in situations in which there is someone, usually Black, to be saved and some-one, usually white, to do the saving (Ahmed, 2004).

Bringing such issues to consciousness enables the space for critical practice to develop further. Silences, gaps, hesitations are of the utmost significance in the development of understanding. These breaks in communication indicate the times and places where a new perspective is breaking through, where there is room for such a new direction to emerge.

Giving and receiving critical feedback: questions, contexts, cues about diversity

Supervision of practitioners in training is a key aspect of professional formation in which critical feedback is given and received. Giving and receiving critical feedback is not easy and it is sometimes therefore avoided.

Discussion Point

Check out the position you are coming from, think about the position other people are coming from, does it hold water–if not why not? (Issitt, 2000)

How do you decide if someone's position holds water?

Supervision is one of the most powerful contexts for the kind of reflective practice outlined above but it is not the only one. The identification of 'critical friends' also enables practitioners to engage in reflection. The question of 'whiteness' was first raised in informal education in the context of the questions raised by practitioners working from a Black perspective. In relation to anti-oppressive practice and a commitment to working across diversity, it is invaluable to draw on the perceptions of practitioners with whom common professional values are shared but whose situation and perspective is clearly different from one's own. A number of models of 'Black and White co-working' and 'male and female co-working' suggest this (Mistry and Brown, 1991). Gaining feedback directly from the group with whom you are working is also important, as material for professional evaluation and reflection.

Common blind spots which have been identified in the struggle to move away from the denial of diversity include avoidance, especially an avoidance of really engaging with people we perceive as 'different'. There is also sometimes a reluctance to respond to the complexities of 'difference'. The people who are perceived as 'different' have their own range of conflicts, their own ways of constructing 'the other' which are not merely a mirror of our own. Finally there is a tendency to assume that non-prejudicial beliefs are already in place in our responses, rather than to actively check out reality. In becoming aware of the limitations as well as the strengths of our own 'situatedness', we can become aware of new possibilities for knowledge and conversation. Knowledge of the world, being up to date, involves reading widely, listening, viewing, accessing the internet, following debates, seeking out alternative points of view. We need to be aware of histories that might matter to young people, particularly the working-class histories, cultural histories and community histories that do not fit with dominant market-based agendas. Informal educators have to be alert to emerging new themes that enable people to make connection with one another.

The sort of questions that can be used in the context of supervision or reflection with a critical friend become part of the conversational repertoire of the youth and community worker. They include open questions, asking about feelings and impressions. Probing and exploratory questions can lead to an the exploration of mirroring and of here and now feelings which pick up on and repeat back the sense that the supervisor is getting from the supervisee: perhaps a sense of uncertainty, or confusion, or stuckness, or feelings of enjoyment and excitement and inspiration.

Taking our time

A number of steps, used systematically, free up space and time for reflection. In particular, regular meeting with a reference/resource group which has been constructed to enable peer reflection from diverse perspectives, and which therefore requires a move 'outside the comfort zone' of everyday practice is recommended. The use of a daily journal with a variety of writing methods, including writing in the third person, methods of free association on significant themes, using metaphors or images opens up creative thinking and creative space. Choose a perspective and imagine the situation from that perspective. It is especially useful in this regard to undertake explorations from the point of view of the least visible or marginalised participants in the situation. Creative thinking arises from provocation and challenge–the challenge to see anew, or to see differently or to change perspective.

In the context of often unrealistically pressurised timescales, taking time for thought is a vital element of creating the space for reflective practice. This involves both creating time and creating spaces, as well as noticing the spaces in which reflection can and does already happen.

It is often at the margins of busy schedules and crowded offices and meeting rooms that such time and space is found. It nevertheless needs to be valued and acknowledged as the creative space which it is. It is through the commitment to setting aside time and withdrawing from the hurly-burly that critical practice can emerge.

What kind of thinking is implied here? Certainly at times it may be analytic thinking, the development of an argument, the pursuit of a deeper understanding through engagement in practice. But, just as often, it is a process of creative thinking which involves seeing and engaging from a new point of view. Change the angle. Develop a vision. Step back. Let go. Allow yourself to be provoked into new ways of seeing and new directions for conversation.

Creative thinking can also enable a vision for practice to emerge–to let through the possibilities implicit in the work, leading towards new forms of practice and possibility. It therefore must involve a deconstruction, a letting go of what exists in the present in order to make room for new forms: a step back from what has been made already in order to see it in a different light, in order to bring about change.

This chapter has emphasised the importance of reflective practice to youth and community workers and has explored what this could mean in the context of power-charged diversity. The case study of a diverse team of women workers working with Black young men highlights the potential for creative practice which arises from systematic reflection. As well as supervision, the use of critical friends or reference groups with diverse perspectives on the work being undertaken is recommended, as is the valuing of space and time for reflection through the use of creative methods of journalling. The act of 'stepping back' creates the space to see work anew.

Key Terms

Supervision and **Critical and reflective practice** are terms used throughout the 'helping professions' to refer to a fundamental professional approach which requires self-awareness and accountability for interventions in the lives of others.

'Race' is placed in inverted commas to refer to the social divisions based on racist evaluations of skin colour and other physical markers or on racist constructions of cultural difference. Other important concepts such as **transcultural** and **power-charged diversity** relate to this context in which 'race', along with other aspects of identity, is constructed as a significant difference through which power relationships are established.

Further Reading

Haraway, D. (1991b) 'Reading Buchi Emecheta', in *Simians, Cyborgs and Women: The Reinvention of Nature*. London: Free Association Books. Donna Haraway's work explores the changing nature of power in a networked world. This essay introduces the concept of 'power-charged diversity' in an educational context.

Haug, F. (1987) *Female Sexualisation: Memory Work and Politics*. London: Verso. Frigga Haug's use of personal reflection to explore power relationships–called 'memory work'–is introduced in this book.

Hawkins, P. and Shohet, R. (2003) *Supervision in the Helping Professions*. Maidenhead: Open University Press. A very useful general introduction to supervision.

Milner, M. (1986) *A Life of One's Own*. London: Virago. An inspiring account of journal-keeping as a source of discovery.

Part I

Whose Agenda?
Reflection Points

- Conversation. When did you last have a conversation with a young person which lasted more than ten minutes?
- Identity. How would you describe your own identity? Complete a sentence starting 'I am ...' ten times. And then another ten times. Complete a sentence starting 'I am not ...'
- Think of the people you see on a day-to-day basis, at work and at home. In what ways do you see them as like you, sharing aspects of your identity? In what ways do you see them as unlike you, having different identities from yours?
- Write down 20 stereotypes you are aware of existing about the people with whom you work. Choose one of them and think of how someone you know who is affected by it.
- Do you keep a practice diary? What kind of writing does it contain?
- Power. What kinds of power are available to you, to share with young people or use in your work with them? What creates the limitations on what you can offer them?
- What are the policy drivers which are providing the funding for the work you are doing? How are young people seen by this policy?
- What aspects of young people's lives and which groups of young people are rendered invisible by these policy agendas?
- How do you check out the position you are coming from? The position other people are coming from? Does it hold water?
- When you reflect on your practice who do you talk to? How diverse are your sources of feedback, your partners in critical reflection?

Part II

Getting to Know Young People

Understanding Young People

- Models of the transition from childhood to adulthood help youth and community workers make sense of how to start their engagement with young people. Social research on the 'youth divide' describes both extended and 'fast-track' transitions.
- Peer groups may offer a form of 'transitional attachment'.
- Adolescence involves a new negotiation of public space and ways of being in public space.
- Sexuality is an important aspect of identity-formation. Models which assume normative gender and heterosexual relationships are critiqued. Such critiques are shared by models of Black identity-formation which emphasise coming to voice rather than biologically determined changes.
- The danger of constructing new norms and 'closure' rather than openness of identities is inherent in all such models.

Being young, no longer a child and not yet an adult, is complicated. At least this is what most theoretical accounts of adolescence suggest. Whether it is understood as a developmental stage, a transition or a renegotiation of space, adolescence is tricky. This chapter discusses the use youth and community workers might make of theories of adolescence at the start of an informal education process, at a time when they are listening, observing and analysing, attending to the young people, seeking to answer the questions: Who are these young people? Why are they *here*? Why are *they* here? (Davies, 2005).

Those who oppose the use of such models argue that they simply fuel the process through which informal education with young people becomes problem-centred rather than person-centred, starting from deficits rather than from strengths. To a young person 'adolescence' is a here-and-now state, 'adolescenthood', as present to them as 'adulthood' is to an adult (Davies, 2000). Theories and models then act as a very rough map, offering clues about what may be found there.

Models of adolescence that suggest fixed and invariant developmental stages which must be passed through can indeed be worse than useless, designed as they are to detect normality and deviance, health and illness. In the context of schooling, such models, with their associated scales and indicators, are the source of much-criticised pathologising. Universal models tend to divert attention from the specific histories and cultures which are of the first importance to informal educators. Nevertheless, this chapter briefly introduces some important concepts which offer clues for those involved in youth work.

Youth: the transition from child to adult

Two powerful discourses have shaped ideas about the nature of children. The first suggests that human nature, and therefore the child, is 'wild' or 'savage' and needs to be tamed and conformed to the rules of society. The second represents the child as naturally benevolent and open to learning, but subject to the violence and oppression of adult society and therefore in need of protection from it. Children are seen as 'little angels' or 'little devils'.

The lives and deaths of real, historically and geographically situated children (especially those whose deaths are tragically caught in the glare of the media) are shadowed by and caught up in these angelic and demonic discourses (Valentine, 2004). When we see someone young for example as 'angelic' and as a potential innocent victim of random violent forces, their closeness to childhood is emphasised. On the other hand, people of the same age who are perpetrators of violence are likely to be depicted not as 'children' but as 'youth' and therefore closer to adults both in their status and in responsibility for their threatening behaviour.

In contrast with 'childhood', adulthood is an altogether more compromised state. Adulthood and childhood are defined in relation to and to a certain extent against one another. Adulthood can be seen as a perspective, a stance towards children. Youth is a transitional state between these perspectives. Children are dependent, while adults are independent. Children are growing in competence; adults have achieved competence. Those who make successful transitions to adulthood, however extended these may be, have paid work or other independent income. They have their own home and they establish their own independent family relationships.

Adolescence as transition

Social research on the transition from childhood to adulthood

Work on youth transitions suggesting a powerful 'youth divide' has shown that there has been a gradual extension in the period of 'youth' (Jones, 2002) and that there are significant differences between groups of young people. In particular there is a growing divide between young people who stay on in education and gain qualifications, and those who leave school at 16 or 17. For this second group, there is a serious risk that they will gain only the lowest-paid jobs and face periods of unemployment. Poorer prospective students may be put off by financial considerations from applying to universities. The prospect of debt frightens some.

Those who have 'broken' or 'fast track' transitions—in particular people who are termed NEETS—are deemed at risk of social exclusion and, as was discussed in Chapter 4, policy attention is focused on them. The meanings and experiences attached to their sexual behaviour, their social networks, their civic participation, or lack of it, their drug use and/or their potential for involvement in anti-social behaviour are closely scrutinised. In contrast with such scrutiny, critical practice in informal education recognises that the meanings associated with transition can be explored by *all* young people, even when, in a highly individuated and reflexive society, the transition seems to happen in individualised and highly internalised ways. Youth work can explore the meanings associated with finding employment, compared to those of the parent generation.

There is also increasingly polarisation between the majority who defer parenthood and the minority who start their families early. This polarisation is largely class based. There are continuing divides based on gender and ethnicity. Even when, for examples, girls from all social groups or boys from ethnic minorities do well in school, this does not confer equality in terms of pay or access to good jobs.

Youth workers can explore the different meanings associated with work, home, travel and leisure for young people whose transitions to 'adulthood' are increasingly seen as 'problematic' because they are 'fast-track'. It has been suggested that the messages they receive from families and communities about these things are based on a perception of a social world as it once was rather than as it now is. For example, working-class young men once valued and aspired to what they saw as a 'proper job'. They still thought in terms of manual jobs, and they had no sense at all that they might not be able to achieve and maintain the traditional pattern of working-class life in which the man was the main breadwinner (Jones, 2002).

The meanings associated with becoming a partner, forming a sexual relationship and becoming a mother or father are also changing. What was previously a middle-class pattern of an extended period of change when different aspects of the transition to independence are tackled in turn is now a majority pattern. We do not know whether people are positively choosing to have children later in their lives, or whether lack of resources and the demands of mortgages and expensive lifestyles cause them to defer family formation. The problems created in the long run by the fact that young people are remaining childless for longer may be greater than those posed by teenage pregnancy. Meanwhile, however, for the minority who become parents at a young age, there are real risks of social exclusion. The importance of access to sex education, contraception and abortion is emphasised by research. The question of how young men make sense of their role as fathers, beyond the notion of financial responsibility, needs to be addressed. There is insufficient awareness of variations in family patterns of care and support, and of times when family support needs to be supplemented with alternative forms of support. Such intergenerational questions have widespread importance and not only for those at risk of exclusion, as young people and the parent and grandparent generations learn to make sense of the new patterns.

Adolescence: inner space and adolescent peer groups

The concept of transition is not only used to make sense in relation to the social roles which young men and young women come to occupy in work, household and family. It is also a significant concept in psychologies of adolescence (Erikson, 1968; Winnicott, 1971), which stress the emotional space of the adolescent transition, particularly those spaces which open up between the attachments of infancy and childhood and the potential future attachments of adult life.

Even when much is in place to support a young person in terms of employment, education and training, it remains important to pay attention to the way in which broken transitions can occur at the level of inner life. Experiences of isolation and depression, of suicidal feelings, of the doldrums, of intense engagement with extremes of life and death are not uncommon. All this suggests that the notion of transition applies to what is happening *within* as well as between selves.

Just as the infant seeks a transitional object as a bridge between the mother and external reality, as a means of adjusting in the early months of life to the necessary separation from the mother, so the adolescent too needs to find transitional attachment to facilitate the separation from parents and into adult status. Such transitional attachments frequently take the form of attachment to a peer group, possibly one with very different values from those available within the family. Whatever form the attachment to a peer group takes, such groups have a strong influence on the formation of adult identity, of adult masculinities and femininities.

Most young people probably identify not with 'subcultures' but, more familiarly, with their town or neighbourhood. Some early commentators saw youth cultures as forms of resistance, structured into the power relationships of the wider society and offering a critique of it.

Other commentators suggest that the question of 'what is being resisted' in the rituals of consumption which mark out peer groups and subcultures is less and less clear. There is no mainstream. There are many streams. Diversity is to be celebrated and antagonism forgotten (Bennett and Kahn-Harris, 2004).

The construction of cultures by and among groups of young people is a significant site for informal education intervention. The question of who such cultures include and who they exclude, which ways of being in the world they validate and which they denigrate, is a question that needs to be critically attended to by youth and community workers.

> When disaffected adolescents from the inner city, more particularly when disaffected, inner city unemployed adolescents resort to symbolic and actual violence, they are playing with the only power at their disposal: the power to discomfit. The power, that is, to pose. (Hebdige, 1988: 17–36)

Transition from child to adulthood: space and the negotiation of public space

Recent work on the sociologies and social geographies of childhood has drawn attention to the question of how public space is imagined by and for adults and children (Valentine, 2004). Children are most at risk in private space, rather than in public space. They are much more likely to be assaulted by people they know than by strangers. They are also at risk from domestic hazards and accidents. Yet parental fears are fuelled by imaginations of stranger danger in public space.

This myth of 'stranger danger' does not only operate in urban space. There are powerful imaginations of rural demons–of 'new age travellers', 'gypsies' and 'walkers'–which keep rural children indoors even when they have wide open spaces all around them (Valentine, 2004).

In educational settings, there has been great reluctance to discuss with children the existence of risk to them within families. At the same time, public safety initiatives have focused on 'stranger danger' campaigns. Valentine argues that this produces public space as 'naturally' and 'normally' adult space in which children are at risk from deviant others (Valentine, 2004: 18). Furthermore, this marking of space is gendered. The male body is saturated with threat and danger; the female body is marked as safe and also potentially vulnerable.

Young men and young women mark the transition from childhood to adulthood through a negotiation of public space, and in doing so seek out new meanings and new spaces, as well as resistance, both conscious and unconscious, to the ways in which adult hegemony has drawn the boundaries around their use of space. Such negotiations are marked by gender, cultural hegemony and access to social capital and material resources which enable mobility. The negotiation of public space is much easier for young people whose families have access to material and cultural resources to enable them to travel and to engage in socially approved activities. However, for all young people, during these negotiations of the public world it is possible, even likely, that new identities will emerge.

Studies of the use of public space by young people in cities suggest that there has been a decline in its use in the last decade, particularly among younger teenagers. This applies equally in the countryside, despite the prevailing image of rural childhoods as idyllic, although this is considerably less studied. Good public space for growing up in promotes a feeling of social activity and social acceptance. It offers varied and interesting settings for activities and a general sense of safety and freedom of movement, as well as peer gathering places. Green areas for informal play and association as well as spaces for organised sports are important. A good public environment for young people depends to a large extent on a cohesive sense of community identity. To the extent that public space becomes associated with exclusion and stigma it becomes a negative space for young people, very often associated with boredom, with fear of crime and harassment, with heavy traffic and with uncollected rubbish and litter.

As public space becomes more and more inhospitable and frightening for young people, the use of curfews and dispersal orders indicates the extent to which young people in public space are thought to be 'up to no good' merely by virtue of their presence. They become objects of public fear and scrutiny. Parks become associated with abuse of civil society; graffiti and vandalism, under-age drinking, gathering in groups can all be seen as challenges and resistances to adult society. This resistance has been responded to by the use of curfews and dispersal orders. Curfews however cannot be shown to have any significant effect on crime levels and it can be argued that they divert police energies into dealing with legitimate adolescent behaviour and away from serious crime (Jeffs and Smith, 1996b; Smithson and Flint, 2006).

One group of young people have been a particular focus of the policing of urban space. Skateboarders have encountered a politics of space similar to the politics of space which affects the experiences of homeless people.

> Like homeless people, skateboarders occupy urban space without engaging in the eco-
> nomic activity of its interiors, to the annoyance of building owners and managers. As a
> result, the urban managers have declared skaters as trespassers, or cited the marks
> skateboarding causes as proof of criminal damage. (Borden, 1998: 2)

Detached youth workers have developed a number of projects with skaters which recognise the importance of skating as a way of occupying urban space. Sometimes however it becomes part of new forms of urban governance which simultaneously involve young people while responding to them as part of a 'crime and disorder' strategy. Young people themselves meanwhile suggest that they do not search out spaces for skating either because of 'disorderliness' or their potential contribution to good civic order and citizenship but on the grounds of their accessibility, sociability, compatibility and the opportunity they offer for tricks (Woolley and Johns, 2001; Stratford, 2002).

Transition from child to adult: sexuality and other identities

Powerful frameworks for adult identity come to be established at this age, and these include the development of the capacity for adult sexual relationships. In the past, discussions of the adolescent transition took for granted the assumption that the move from childhood to adulthood involved the natural and normal acquisition of heterosexuality. Now such assumptions are very much open to question: the normal and the natural are not what they once seemed.

It is more than twenty years since Carol Gilligan demonstrated the masculine bias of Lawrence Kohlberg's work on moral development (Gilligan, 1982). Against models which suggested a universal goal of 'autonomy' Gilligan went on to posit an alternative 'female model' of development in which the goal of autonomy is less significant than the goal of connectedness, of 'being in relation'. However, Gilligan's work can be seen as itself remaining profoundly normative and grounded in an essentialist and reductive account of femininity. It has been critiqued as such from lesbian perspectives, for example (Tronto, 1993).

In recognition of this, several writers have offered models of gay identity formation and lesbian identity formation which depart from the normative models of heterosexuality. In a similar vein to Gilligan's critique of Kohlberg, gay writers also offered their critique of James Marcia's work on identity formation. Cass (1979) suggested Identity Confusion, Identity Comparison, Identity Tolerance, Identity Acceptance, Identity Pride and Identity Synthesis as stages in the 'coming out' process for gay men. More recently, lesbian writers have developed models of lesbian identity formation which suggest that, once achieved, it is a more secure identity than heterosexual identity for many women, and they too have used James Marcia's model to critique the normative assumptions of heterosexuality (Kitzinger and Wilkinson, 1995). These critics of models of identity formation rooted in biology emphasise in contrast the importance of the emergence of voice and the enabling of voices to be heard.

From the 1980s onwards, the project to uncover submerged voices and hidden experiences became more widely acknowledged and supported. In particular, the dominance of white Eurocentric and Anglo-American models became the subject of critique just as the dominance of the 'heterosexual assumption' had been. Whereas Gilligan had attempted, at first, to ground her account of sexual difference and of the different feminine road to development in claims about essential (biological) gender difference, post-colonial, anti-racist and 'queer' thinkers were more inclined to focus on the historical conditions of oppression in which identity emerges for Black people and for lesbian and gay people. On this basis, a number of writers have offered typologies and 'models of development' which in some ways parallel those offered by developmental psychologists. Any group which has been 'othered' by normative models has the potential to create and offer its own model in response, with the concomitant danger that it, in turn, creates a norm.

In relation to Black identity formation, the nigrescence model associated with W.E. Cross has been particularly important and widely discussed. Cross (1980) suggests a five stage movement, through the transformation from pre-encounter to internalisation/commitment. Inspired by Fanon, Cross describes the movement from pre-encounter to encounter with hostile perceptions which then precipitates an intense search for Black identity. The third stage immersion-emersion glorifies Blackness and denigrates whiteness. The fourth stage, internalisation, allows the person to focus on things other than him/herself in relation to his/her ethnic group, and the fifth stage (in parallel with Marcia's account of 'identity achievement') suggests that the person finds activities and commitments to express his/her new identity.

This model forms an almost direct parallel to the account of the 'coming out' process for lesbians and gay men. The dangers of such models are perhaps highlighted by this fact. Whilst it may be true that responses to pejorative labelling follow a predictable path and can have more or less positive outcomes for individuals responding to such labels, it is also the case that expecting someone to conform their responses to a particular pattern or model (seen as the 'healthy' model) can be oppressive in its turn.

Alongside and in tension with such developments, critical psychologists who reject the framework of developmental psychology as inevitably normative point to the possibility of exploring the process of becoming a subject, the process of identity-formation, as always complex, contradictory and open. The very notion of 'identity' itself is one which prematurely closes off the future, and the processes and practices which enable resistance to identity formation may be as important as the practices which promote the formation of a secure and boundaried ego.

From the point of view of critical psychology it is the conditions which enable something new to emerge which are of interest. Such theorists are often as interested in *hybridity* as they are in identity, in the notion of 'queer' with all its productivity, in the non-white–as they are in establishing a positive sense of identity and community. Rejection of categories, boxes and labels as constraining rather than enabling is a significant aspect of such theorisations. A sense of 'difference' is a signal of the way forward rather than a threat to commonality. Solidarity and community represent a form of coercion to such theorists. Networks replace communities as the model of connectedness (Dean, 1996; Tate, 2005).

Connecting back to the youth work conversation

All the accounts of transition discussed so far in this chapter have something important to say to informal educators working with young people. They can contribute to an answer to the questions: Who are these young people? Why are they *here*? Why are *they* here?

Who are these young people?

The young people are male and female; what difference does that make to their aspirations and their possibilities in relation to work, to education, to family, to life? They are at particular ages–what difference does it make, economically, socially, emotionally, sexually, that some are 13 and some are 17 and some are 21? They come from particular backgrounds or communities; so what sort of messages about themselves and their opportunities are they getting? They attend or don't attend particular schools, colleges or workplaces. How are they treated? Do they like school or college or work? They are skaters, townies, Goths, casuals, scallies. They are Muslims, Catholics, Church of God of Prophecy, doing the 'silver ring thing', listening to rap, listening to indie. They support United. They support City. They are depressed. They are troublesome. They have girlfriends; boyfriends; lovers. They must wait till they are married. They hide their sexuality. They are young people with disabilities and don't access the city centre. They are called by their names: Arjam, Wesley, Hussein, Charlene, Paul, David, Dominic, Mary, Emily, Tembi, Akosa, Maryam, Miriam, Khatidja, Naim, Mark, Angelina.

Why are *they* here?

Why are these young people here, rather than others? Are the others all well occupied somewhere else? Or are the others frightened to come here because of who might be here? Are there boys here and therefore not girls? Are there boys and girls here and therefore the gay young men are not visible? Are they here because they can get here under their own steam, they aren't relying on anyone else for transport, their disability doesn't prevent them going out much?

Have they chosen this in preference to the TV, the computer screen, the music lesson, the sports team commitment? Does their presence here mean that other young people will not arrive, will perhaps be afraid to come? Or have these young people found a safe space here? Are they here because of the enjoyment that they find in one another's company? Or because they don't want to be left out? Are they here because they've been told to be–on a school exclusion order or a court order? Are they here because they have come with their friend?

Why are they *here*?

Perhaps this group of young people has nowhere else to go? They are pushing the boundaries and have been placed on a curfew, or on a dispersal order and they have been moved on to new places, just outside the dispersal zone. Perhaps this is a warm and well lit space, full of commercial leisure provision and, although they have limited money, it feels a safe space to be. Perhaps this is the only lesbian and gay support group for miles around and they are frightened that someone will see them coming in. Perhaps they are here because it's a place that their parents know about and that makes them feel safe. They are here because they want to be here, they have agreed with one another and the worker to come here. They are here because it is neutral territory. Not on any one group's turf. They are here and hoping for something.

Key Terms

Extended transition and **Fast-track transition** are terms for the period of life between childhood and adulthood: they have been coined by a sociologist to account for the evidence of a 'youth divide' and of the changing time frame of adolescence.

Transitional space refers to both the physical space which the young occupy and also to a psychological space in which the possibility of development and change emerges.

As well as the negotiation of peer groups, **Identity formation** as a task of adolescence refers to the work of imagination and of 'coming to voice' as analysed in a number of 'alternative' models of development.

Further Reading

Griffin, C. (1993) *Representations of Youth: The Study of Youth and Adolescence in Britain and America*. Cambridge: Polity. An important analysis of the impact of different theoretical frameworks on either pathologising or enabling a more emancipatory approach to understanding young people.

Henderson, S., Holland, J., McGrellis, S., Sharpe, S. and Thomson, R. (2007) *Inventing Adulthoods: a Biographical Approach to Youth Transitions*. London: Sage. This longitudinal study shows how a holistic approach to young people which transcends the sociology/psychology divide can work.

McDonald, R. and Marsh, J. (2005) *Disconnected Youth? Growing Up in Britain's Poor Neighbourhoods*. Basingstoke: Palgrave. A good account of the experience of fast-track transitions.

Valentine, G. (2004) *Public Space and the Culture of Childhood*. London: Ashgate. An important account of the spatial construction of youth as 'threat'.

7

Boundaries in Practice

- The question of where, how and by whom boundaries are drawn is an essential question. Professional boundaries–against sexual intimacy and against violence and discrimination–create safe space for young people.
- Boundaries are both physical–to do with places; and psychological–to do with relationships and networks. They are full of meaning.
- Close attention to the existing conversations of groups enables youth workers to understand the meaning of particular boundary negotiations and border conflicts. Some boundaries are negotiable and some are non-negotiable. They can shift and change. Positive action by youth workers can lead to a change in boundaries.

Where does youth work happen?

The professional boundaries which the informal educator establishes are a prerequisite of the 'safe spaces' for conversation. The buildings, streets and open spaces in which youth work happens carry meaning. They offer physical boundaries to practice. The psychological boundaries between groups provide a starting point for youth work conversations. Attention to such borders and boundaries suggests directions for continuing conversation.

Case Study

Different groups of students use the spaces in the canteen in different ways. There are choices about who to sit with over food, over drinks, and who to stand outside with over cigarettes. When it is Ramadan as the autumn term starts, there will in all probability be a group of British Asian men, all Muslim students, who hang out together away from the canteen. There will be one or two Muslim women with them, creating a space away from the food and drink. At other times of year, the college canteens are a good neutral space for young Asian men to connect with each other, and with others, a good place to hang out, a safe space to be. Safe, even to the extent that the canteen rather than the classroom becomes the hub of activity. Another group of boys plays football in the gym.

During the school day, there are places in the shops where school students gather, away from the school environment, near enough to register for lessons, far away enough to provide a place to smoke away from adult eyes. In the local park there is, allegedly, a space where the college and school students go further to smoke cannabis. There are two parks, so it's important to know which park it is. One of the parks leads out towards the river, and it's there that courting couples are to be found, making a break from the crowd, looking for some peace and quiet and for some secrecy or privacy.

Streets that are empty of young people in the mornings are full of young people at 2.30 a.m., as people leave parties or clubs and make their way home. This is a student city.

Which young people can come out to these places? Which ones are still at home? Who connects with others privately, using the mobile phone for texting or making the internet, virtual space, their chief and safest space?

Professional boundaries: ground rules for safe practice and the law

Working informally makes attention to the informal educator's own boundaries and relationship to the law and to the authorities, particularly to the police, an issue.

By professional boundaries I refer to a setting of physical, emotional and ethical limits. For most professionals, 'professional boundaries' are clearly marked by the kinds of spaces they occupy, such as an office, a classroom or a clinic. For informal educators, this is not the case. It may not always be entirely clear what the youth worker's friendliness denotes, leading to an expectation that a worker will 'turn a blind eye' to certain criminal activities or that sensitive information which is private to a young person will not be shared. At or near the beginning of work with a group, committed practitioners will find a way to make these matters clear. They explain or show how they will deal with sensitive information and with matters of law. They also need to communicate clearly their commitment to young people's rights, to their safety and well-being and to non-violence.

From this non-negotiable professional stance, through observation and listening, the worker can come to understand what boundaries mean to the young people they are working with. The practitioner will start to recognise the extent to which they will or will not hear sensitive information from young people. By choosing which boundaries to observe, including making decisions about where and when to accompany the young people they are working with, the youth worker will make choices about what they hear and know about.

There are issues about the safety of the worker as well as the safety of young people. Detached youth work takes place on young people's own ground, in public spaces. Perhaps the youth worker meets up with young people in a well-lit shopping area, a town or city centre or near a leisure complex. However, it may be that young people are moved on from those areas, seen as posing a threat, subject to dispersal orders or curfews. The youth worker needs to make choices about whether to move on with them, recognising those places and times when the young people's activities may be shifting from legality to illegality; in particular recognising a boundary with young people's drug use while keeping open the possibility of informal education conversations about drugs. This means choosing not to be in particular places with young people and being clear about that choice with them.

Informality can make the boundaries of what can and can't be talked about without fear of reprisals unclear. The issue of sharing information needs to be clarified in the context of inter-professional teams and of the common assessment framework in operation in relation to the safeguarding of children. Confidentiality is especially important during adolescence because the competence to make informed decisions about personal safety is at the heart of the transition from childhood to adulthood.

There are some circumstances in which educators working with young people clearly have a responsibility to break confidentiality. In a situation in which there is a serious risk to young people's life, safety or well-being, or that of others, including the lives of younger children, confidentiality must be broken. Youth and community workers must be clear about these circumstances and communicate this to young people with whom they are working. The creation of a safe environment involves the communication of the very clear professional boundaries which youth and community workers have. Making safe space means communicating about ethics. Confidentiality is important, but, if it comes to a choice, preventing serious harm is more important.

Rights-based approaches (as discussed in Chapter 3) create a framework in which it is possible to educate young people about their rights as well as enabling practitioners and young people to be aware of their responsibilities. Recent research suggests that most young people are far more aware of their responsibilities than of their rights (Lister, et al., 2005) and taking a rights-based approach offers a useful basis for establishing ground rules and contracts for working with young people. Alongside an ethic of rights it is necessary to espouse an ethic of care and a sense of the importance of networks of mutuality in order to counter neglect. Underpinning all the practice of youth and community work as informal learning is an ethic of non-violence and non-discrimination (Banks, 1999; Harrison and Wise, 2005).

Ground rules, implicit or explicit, enable conversation to develop. These are revisited in more or less formal ways throughout the period of work with a group. Such ground rules (sometimes called contracts and drawn up formally; at other times understood more organically as 'conditions for working together') will usually include expectations about speaking and listening, about respecting and not judging, about confidentiality and gossip. Others concern openness to change, to recognising mistakes and learning from them, as well as explicit commitment to non-violence and non-discrimination.

The setting of such boundaries establishes a sense of what is negotiable and what is non-negotiable between informal educators and young people, and a sense of where the responsibilities and accountabilities of the youth workers lie, in a way that encourages openness and honesty in conversation from the start. However, the nature of the informal setting makes this a different process from one undertaken in a classroom. It happens naturally, through conversation.

The physical boundaries of public spaces

Time spent at the beginning of a period of work finding out about how public spaces are used in a particular neighbourhood and where young people go is valuable. Some public places are also semi-secret or private places: places where drinking, or drugs, or sex happen; there is a sense of riskiness for workers and young people alike about such places.

If the space in which educators work with young people is one over which the youth and community worker has some control, and in which they can exercise some influence or authority, there is still a need to be observant of the way space in a project base is used by young people, how it is shared by the young people themselves and with other users of that space. If there is a regular pre-school playgroup or an regular elders' lunch club sharing the space that 'belongs' to the young people, who has to put their equipment away? How does the decoration and design of the environment reflect the involvement and participation of young people in particular parts of a community project or, indeed, in particular public spaces in the city or town or village community? So much of the time of many practitioners is concerned with buildings, the opening and locking of them, and the consequences of shared use that they can come to seem a burden rather than a resource for practice.

Sometimes the groups with whom an informal educator develops his or her practice come to him or her; sometimes the informal educator, especially in the role of detached youth worker, moves with them. In either case, the practitioner makes a series of important observations, looking out for the starting points which will enable the conversation to get going.

What's involved in listening? And who gets listened to?

The belief that professionals were not noticing and were not listening to certain groups, particularly so-called 'ethnic minority groups', led, from the 1980s onwards, to the development of 'cultural awareness training' and 'equality and diversity training'. But such 'training' soon became thought of as a potentially dangerous diversion from a more fundamental practice in which all informal educators need to engage: listening, asking and observing. Listening, observing and finding out can and needs to happen with any group the informal educator is working with, whether the educator assumes that he or she is 'similar' to the group or 'different' from them.

Listening and talking where boundaries are crossed

In urban multi-culture boundaries are created not just in the negotiation of space but in patterns of talk which separate insiders from outsiders, and street talk from professional talk (Back, 1996). Young people from all communities have developed shared forms of talk through which they deliberately distance themselves from adults, especially from adult authorities such as teachers, and even youth workers. Such talk is also a way of marking 'insiders' and 'outsiders' within a group of young people. It creates defences against hostility.

Talk is commonly a source of creativity and resistance amongst first and second generation migrants, especially where English is not the mother tongue or the language spoken at home. Forms of speech which are socially stigmatised can become privileged forms of speech among adolescent peer groups. In the 1980s in the UK Jamaican creole/patwa formed the basis of one of the languages most popular with adolescents and it was spoken widely across Black and white communities (Hewitt, 1986). This talk continues its power through the influence of rap, dancehall and ragga-roots. It is now claimed as a language, rather than merely a dialect, by some in Jamaica. The technical term for such languages is 'creolised languages' and they are sometimes referred to as languages of transition. The term 'transition', occurring again in this context, once more points to an understanding of change, particularly the ways in which communities change through migration.

The concept of 'language of transition' suggests a reluctance on the part of the dominated community to abandon altogether their own mother tongues. However, 'creole' languages are also recognised as languages in their own right and have long histories. Their existence as 'transitional languages', languages that exist *between* communities, becomes hidden. For example, Yiddish is a long-established language, yet the vocabulary of Yiddish changed enormously in the Jewish migration to the United States. (The Yiddish word for 'window' changed from 'fenster' to 'vinder' in New York.) When young people use such 'transitional' languages they are mirroring the process of 'crossing' from one community to another and this in turn parallels the process of 'crossing' from child to adult status. Some conversations among young people take place happily in more than one language. They move from Hindi or Gujerati to English and back again. In such movements learning is potentially very rich, so moves to suggest that young people become monolingual should be resisted (Bhaba and Gilman, 2001).

There is also a politics of the protection of languages, often minority ancient languages which are at risk of dying out. The protection of the Welsh language is a good example of this. It is a requirement of all educational provision in Wales, including the provision of youth work, that it includes a minimum amount of Welsh language education. This officially promoted bilingualism sets up different patterns again of talk among young people, in which sometimes English and sometimes Welsh may be a language of resistance.

Some, though not all, informal educators will themselves be bilingual or trilingual and able to engage with young people using their own language resources. All youth workers need to learn to listen very carefully to how changes in language mark changes in group boundaries. When do young people switch codes or register? When do they move out of the dominant common language, used for communicating with a professional, say, and move into one that is more restricted, to themselves or their close friends? It might be that they are moving into talk about music which is immensely significant to them and their identity affiliations. It might be that they are moving into boasting about their sexual encounters; it might be that they are creating terms of abuse. These shifts tell the educator something about a boundary, potentially something about what is most important to the young men and women with whom they are working and what is therefore most to be protected from the interfering gaze of adults. When youth workers are able to engage in such talk as a resource for the conversations, along with connecting with the music and style that matter to the young people they are working with, this forms an enormous resource for practice.

Noticing networks, noticing individuals: paying attention to the boundaries of groups which young people create

Boys, allegedly, tend to form larger primary peer groups than girls and these peer groups contribute to extended networks. In contrast, girls in adolescence, allegedly, tend to form pairs of friends and smaller primary peer groups. It is important for informal educators to consider and learn about the extent of a young person's networks.

Some young people may be leading quite isolated lives. The role of the educator may be to offer access to wider networks. Others may be part of wider networks and the informal educator will work with them, developing conversations from the conversational starting points and preoccupations of primary peer groups and extended social networks. Masculine networks may spread through a wide age range, extending the range of experiences which contribute to the development of cultures within a group of boys. These larger networks may well relate to members of a particular 'tribe'–skinheads, skaters–which the youth workers seek to engage. Observation at the beginning of an informal education process needs to be specific. The youth workers must gather information about the individual young people with whom the project will work: names, and nicknames; contact details; something about their background and community; where they live; whether they live with their parents and what their relationships with their parents/carers are like; how they are relating with one another in a group. Are boys and girls connecting? How are girls connecting with other girls? How are boys connecting with other boys?

Youth workers need to learn how to be nosy without being intrusive, since it is such initial attention to young people's context that enables work to develop creatively. Listening, including asking questions and the ways of asking questions, is well recognised as necessary to the practice of counselling but it is not always recognised as a vital tool of informal education. The quality of attention called for is sometimes called 'deep listening' because it involves attention to the whole of what is happening, not just the content of the communication. It means attending to the significance of what is happening for the people involved, its emotional tone. It involves finding out about where people are coming from and also about where they might dream of going to. It links attention to the here and now to an awareness of what has been and what might be in the future.

There are significant overlaps between the practice of counselling and the practices of informal education. Many 'counselling skills' in relation to listening and conversation are also in another context 'informal education skills'. The purposes of the practices also overlap. In informal education, there is more attention to the overt content of communication, with the purpose of making the links between a growth in personal understanding and wider social development. It could be suggested that while therapy uses the practice of deep listening in order to uncover deep personal patterns, the practice of informal education also engages in deep listening, but in order to make the links between the personal, the social and the political. Youth workers do not engage with young people because of problems they are experiencing but on account of their potential.

The use of open questions and probing is essential to deep listening. Although the youth and community worker who successfully builds up trusting relationships will certainly hear about problems, listening is not primarily problem-focused but develops a sense of the potential of the young people involved in the conversation; it is necessary for the educator to gain as full a picture as possible of the context of the young person's life. In turn this leads to the analysis of generative themes which will support developmental work. Within the notion of 'generative themes' are included the ideas and activities that bring a sparkle to someone's eyes; a feeling of happiness; a sense of striving or struggling with something new. This means being attentive to the conversations which either mark boundaries or mark a desire to cross boundaries, the transitions of language.

Such transitions often suggest that something new is emerging. Attention to what's new and what's interesting is a significant source of informal education. Listening out for the aspects of the culture that most engage young people is central. The youth worker also pays attention to what young people seek to draw boundaries against. They need to understand what happens when young people draw boundaries to protect something they value, or when boundaries are drawn because they wish to distance themselves from someone. Some practitioners describe, not just 'eyes in the back of their head' but also a 'third ear': knowing that there are things you won't be told and what they are about; recognising too that if youth workers put themselves in certain places or conversations they will hear things they may not want to hear.

Shifting boundaries: the practice of positive action

It is often possible for informal educators to take small steps which change or challenge the boundaries of conversations and activities, in a commitment to challenging practices which discriminate. Informal educators also contribute to the development of wider public conversations whose aim is to develop an open, inclusive and non-discriminatory civil society. Small sometimes symbolic actions can change the terms of conversation.

Control of space and resources is a time-honoured way in which dominance can be exercised. Steps which challenge such dominance often appear to 'create conflict'. It might be more accurate to say that they make the conflicts that are already there visible. The conversations which happen when positive action is taken to ensure greater fairness between groups bring to life many feelings of injustice beyond the specific immediate focus of conversation.

Take the example of access to a gym. If, in a setting in which a group of boys has always used the gym to play football, thus excluding girls and other boys, a staff team takes steps to exclude boys football from the gym for particular sessions, in order to hold aerobics or dance or badminton or even a women's football session, the staff will find themselves on the receiving end of a good deal of resentment and anger from those who are displaced.

This is recognised as a consequence of affirmative action, at a public political level as well as at the more everyday level of informal education conversations. Justice and fairness demand that positive steps are taken to address an obvious inequality. But taking such steps leads to grievance on the part of those from whom the resource has been taken, often people who have little enough in the first place. 'It's not fair' is then a common response to steps that have in fact been taken to ensure greater fairness.

What would be fairer? Perhaps to have two gyms. However, the pattern of dominance might easily re-establish itself. Both might become spaces for boys' football, for which there is huge demand. Positive actions, in the context of an unfair system or of systemic dominance, need to be repeated over and over again. This can lead to the curious sense of the group which is marked out for repeated positive action being privileged over other groups. 'The girls are getting all the attention.' It can also lead to a reinforcement of the idea that the group on whose behalf positive steps are taken is oddly deficient, with special needs that have to be catered for over and over again. Positive action can then feed back into a discourse which 'blames the victim' for their disadvantaged position in a system which is stacked against them.

So, in the context of a youth project where a night has been allocated as a 'girls' activities night' it is essential that the informal education process continues with both boys and girls, to discuss why this is happening. Committed practitioners are aware of the resistances that they will meet. It is important to anticipate how the conversation might develop after the first step has been taken: the 'it's not fair' which leads to further talking and new opportunities for the young women who are included and for the young men who feel excluded and that they are losing out. 'Why does fairness matter?' 'What else could we do?' 'What are the things you're never encouraged to try?' 'Is it easier for girls to try "boyish" things than for boys to try "girlie" things?' And why is that? 'Do boys still worry that someone will think they are homosexual if they aren't playing football?' Such conversations, investigations and questions take place over a long period of time and are then in their turn accompanied by new actions, including actions which provide new and non-traditional opportunities to boys.

Positive action is undertaken when challenging the segregation of communities. 'Tuesday night is a white night.' 'This is a white area.' 'This is an Asian area.' 'Keep off our turf.' Such boundaries can be policed at one extreme by criminal gangs and gang leaders with all their hierarchies and control. But they can also be maintained by seemingly polite middle-class social norms which exclude by saying nothing: the silence reported by many a Black youth worker who has entered a country pub during a residential and attempted to buy a drink can also speak volumes about who is or is not expected to occupy the space.

Paradoxically, the most successful examples of activities which challenge enforced or taken for granted segregation have been in programmes which have another primary focus. Programmes and events with a theme of creativity have been very successfully used as a focus to bring groups together. A condition of funding for cultural work for example can be that projects bring groups together who would ordinarily work separately. The conversations that then occur are in part about the arts project in hand: but in part such conversations enable learning across communities. Using methods, including games and icebreakers, which assist participants in overcoming politeness/and inhibition/fear of insult, all of which stand in the way of learning, is a vital skill for such work.

It must not be imagined that such challenges to segregation can be undertaken without resistance. The commitment to keeping groups separate can be strong, and can provoke violent actions when group boundaries are challenged. Initiatives to cross boundaries are often actively discouraged by power-holders in particular groups, especially by community leaders who may sense a threat to their power. The possibility of and fear of so-called 'mixed' relationships is often what is at stake here. The desire on the part of male 'leaders' to control women in a group can also be part of the drawing of boundaries and the resistance to crossing them. Much resistance is at the level not of conversation but of control through the use of language to denigrate and humiliate, and to create potential targets for attack. Specific individual young people, perhaps particularly young women, who do not conform to group rules and choose to move between groups, are often subject to vilification and attack.

Formal highly boundaried spaces are therefore often safer spaces for anti-segregation work than the places of everyday negotiations. Residentials away from community settings as well as schools and colleges have offered neutral spaces. These are places where mixing might begin to happen, even when it is discouraged by the keepers of community boundaries. Informal educators may need to be prepared to move into more formal settings in order for such work to occur.

This chapter has been concerned with the framework of boundaries with which young people live; and the framework of professional boundaries within which youth workers must seek to operate. The boundaries we are referring to are to do with speech and listening and therefore with ethics. They are to do with the law. They are also boundaries of space and place. They mark places of exclusion or places of potential crossing and change. Creativity in taking positive action to challenge boundaries has been identified as a source of youth work conversations. It is from the negotiation of these boundaries that much that is creative in the beginning of informal education practice occurs.

Key Terms

Boundaries and what happens at them are important in a range of disciplines, from psycho-analysis to geography. Boundaries set limits and are important because they create safe space and a sense of security. 'Good fences make good neighbours.' At the same time, migrations happen, boundaries are crossed and the crossing of them makes new identities possible.

Listening which is active and non-judgmental and full of curiosity, asking open questions and probing questions is sometimes a fundamental of good practice in informal learning. Listening is the partner of speaking and voice, since for voices to connect to power, they need to be heard.

Positive action refers to actions which are taken to strengthen the position of groups of young people who are resisting discrimination, in strategies which promote equality.

Further Reading

Back, L. (1996) *New Ethnicities and Urban Culture: Racisms and Multiculture in Young Lives*. London: UCL Press. An analysis of the negotiations of 'race' and identities in an urban setting, including in a youth club.

Factor, F., Chauhan, V. and Pitts, J. (2001) *The RHP Companion to Working with Young People*. Lyme Regis: Russell House. A good source on a number of forms of positive action in youth work.

Geldard, D. and Geldard, K. (1999) *Counselling Adolescents: The Pro-active Approach*. London: Sage. Very good on forms of 'open questioning'.

8

'It's Boring…' How Do Youth Workers Engage?

- Everyday chat forms a basis for developing relationships. Dissatisfaction, disrespect and boredom are important starting points.
- Youth workers challenge boredom by taking an interest in young people, looking for what will spark an interest, what creates greater expectations and goes beyond the everyday.
- Some young people create interest and excitement by provoking conflict or rehearsing prejudices and put-downs. Youth workers can move such conversations on in creative ways.

Just chatting

'It's boring.' 'It's boring round here.' 'There's nothing to do round here.' Or, 'There's always something happening.' 'It's a laugh.' The buzz of the group or the flatness and the lack of stimulus in over-familiar company are significant starting points. There is such a thing as too much routine, parks that are too cold on a winter and even a summer evening. 'There isn't enough to do round here.' This familiar complaint provides a clear opening for youth work. The beginning of many informal education sessions is in chat. Chat and everyday contact provide the point of engagement for later, purposeful conversations (Wolfe, 2001).

Some of the time such chat is the glue of a relationship, the communication that creates connection without very much in the way of meaning. It's simply a matter of keeping the chat going. This will be about relatively impersonal topics and common points of reference. Popular TV is a widely recognised topic for such conversations. Such chat functions to create a bond of warmth and connection. It establishes a light level of interaction and exchange. It has some easily recognisable conversational features, such as turn-taking and the exchange of stories. By turn-taking participants in talk follow on from one another, include or exclude one another. In the exchange of stories, conversational participants become familiar with one another's reference points. At the beginning it can be as simple as finding out about what TV programmes someone watches regularly, what football teams they support, what other sport they follow, what music they are listening to. The stories they tell about what has been happening at school or college or work or at home, the characters who appear regularly, offer clues to further conversations.

This chatting also enables the educator to create a picture of who these young people are, who maintain the energy of the group and who are on the edges of it, and what the terms of the conversation are. 'Light and chatty conversations' move into light and chatty but more serious conversations and sometimes to a long-term engagement at a group or one-to-one level (Spence and Devanney, 2007).

Listening for: dissatisfaction

While this chat is happening, important cues, if they are picked up by the youth worker, enable a deeper connection. Dissatisfaction and discontent are invaluable allies of the practitioner. It is important to attempt to understand their source. Such feelings are not always freely expressed, but when they are, even when it is with negativity, hate and anger, they need to be acknowledged and worked with. Powerful feelings of hurt and fear can often be found underlying anger. The sense that 'This place is rubbish' can contain a strong feeling of hurt that the people who come to this place are themselves regarded as rubbish. The committed practitioner can acknowledge such feelings and recognise the need to make a change, to create a place in which people feel welcomed and valued, in which their worth and dignity is recognised. Young people may feel many places to be welcoming, even when they are in desperate need of repair. And even a smart place can seem hostile, if the people there are unwelcoming.

Case Study

In one club, said to be integrated, the scene was chaotic and disorganised. Young people with disabilities were present in considerable numbers, but neither integration nor youth work were observed. A fight was going on at a pool table with cues used as weapons. Noone seemed to take responsibility for this behaviour and it was some minutes before the worker eventually intervened. The young victim had learning difficulties and some mobility problem. In the same club some young people sat around unoccupied with catalogues on their laps, and other young people passing them would pat them on the head and continue on their way with no attempt at communication. Others were called by unflattering nicknames. The situation illustrated lack of understanding by both staff and young people.

Youth Work with Young People with Disabilities: A Report (HMI, 2001)

The immediate environment is often the subject of dissatisfaction. In comparison with much commercial provision, publicly provided facilities for young people (especially in the poorest neighbourhoods) historically became shabby and unwelcoming. Much effort and investment continues to be needed to challenge this state of disrepair. Buildings may be in a remote part of an estate or of a campus. They may not promote a feeling of security or safety. Alternatively, they may have the appearance of a high security lock-up.

Regeneration projects have made a difference in some areas to the physical spaces available for use by youth and community workers. Significant numbers of young people have been involved in the creation of new accommodation and new spaces, including the provision of comfortable and attractive furniture and decoration.

Serious neglect of young people's interests has led, in some places and at times, to attacks on youth centres as well as schools, during 'disturbances' as well as in more isolated and 'delinquent' acts of arson. Such attacks have come as no surprise to youth and community workers, who suggest that the quality of the building and the facilities speaks volumes about what the young people of particular neighbourhoods (and also the staff) are deemed to be worth. Neglected facilities, as well as facilities inaccessible to young people on account of their cost, can encourage a different turn of conversation: towards the question of what would be involved in self and community respect.

Listening for: adult disrespect

Dissatisfaction is also commonly expressed with adult 'authorities' with whom young people are or, more frequently, are not in contact: school, police, security guards. The lack of respect they are perceived to have for young people is a starting point for conversation. It is essential that youth workers hear this dissatisfaction as it may be a source of energy and development.

It may allow anger and power struggles to be readily and safely articulated. It may be easier to express conflict with relatively insignificant adults in public positions than to express and experience conflict with adults in a young person's family. There is a common pattern of assumptions in schools and among adults generally that the 'authorities' 'know what is going on' without needing to bother to listen or explore. So, a young man who always wears 'hoodies' is likely to find himself the object of suspicion as soon as he goes into a shop. It is assumed by adults that because he is wearing a particular local uniform, he is likely to be a shoplifter. He has to modify his behaviour to ensure that he is not suspected of having stolen anything. School is also a place in which a lack of respect is frequently reported. The apparently arbitrary application of rules rather than a more adult negotiation of relationships is a frequent source of a sense of disrespect.

Such forms of frustration can become flashpoints of anger. They reveal a failure to recognise young people's desires to be treated as young adults, even during the period of adolescence when they have yet to become fully adult. Part of the youth and community worker's role is to find or to create the channels of communication through which anger and its associated needs can be expressed. In doing this the informal educator moves the chat on to a deeper level of conversation.

Listening for: boredom and what's interesting

Dissatisfaction is frequently not expressed. Instead it is covered over by the flatness of boredom, that strange state of disengagement which can be both a defence and a protection against change.

Boredom operates as a defence against change, when the tensions and contradictions of life may be suggesting to an individual that either a change in their circumstances or a change in their approach to their circumstances is required. It may also protect against insistent demands from others that a person recognise the need to change. When there is dominance or manipulation occurring in a conversation, boredom can also become sullenness, a 'dumb insolence' which resists attempts at manipulation. To be bored can be oddly all consuming. Boredom can offer a container, provide a boundary to keep in check many of the contradictions, tensions and antagonisms of life. It 'keeps the lid on' things. It is sometimes referred to as 'being in the doldrums'.

The 'doldrums' is a part of the ocean in which sailing boats cannot make progress on their journey because of the complicated and contradictory winds, which leave them unable to move. Boredom is sometimes a way of expressing a state in which a person or a group of people is prevented from accessing the energies associated with the contradictory ways the winds of change are blowing in their life. Such boredom, connected to a kind of adolescent moodiness, is a transitional space that has its own purpose, its own character that needs to be attended to. The yawn of boredom witnesses to a weariness, a tiredness that comes from containing the mixed and turbulent and contradictory feelings, even the very intense life–death struggles of adolescence. To be bored may be a protection against being stimulated, engaged, ready to move and to move on, ready to challenge the established group boundaries and the constructed identities which are on offer. To be bored may be safer and less risky than to be interested.

Nevertheless, it is essential that the informal educator provoke risk-taking, seek engagement, seek to discover 'what's interesting' and harness all the enthusiasm and curiosity they can. In discovering 'what's interesting' the educator gets personal, engaging with what matters to particular individuals and taking an interest in them as people.

Listening for: I get a kick out of winding you up ...

Wind-ups are a common way that some young people create a buzz of excitement and gain the attention of adults. Joking is also a way that some practitioners start conversations. Humour is a way of developing a connection. It is an important vehicle through which young people establish connections among themselves.

One form of humorous wind-up or teasing takes the form of banter and boasting, boasting about particular macho exploits, whether sexual or aggressive or both. This banter, traditionally associated with some masculine speech, also extends to include girls. Both girls and boys can find themselves giving out or positioned as the target of the banter. Such banter has been studied in relation to sexual name-calling, such as the use of the labels of 'slappers' and 'slags' but it can extend to a whole range of derogatory name-calling (Lees, 1983).

Given that the ethics of youth and community work involves a commitment to non-violence and non-discrimination, the use of such put-downs is an almost fail-safe way of gaining the attention of a worker, if only in the form of attempts to regulate such talk. The wind-up of workers is a form of engagement. Negative attention is better than none.

Such conversations can be places of excitement as well as fear and danger. 'What's interesting' sometimes emerges in the form of wind-ups which reveal prejudice and potential violence. Young people, including young men, are more likely to be victims of prejudice and violence than to be its perpetrators. Committed practitioners will be aware of their own prejudices and the roots of such prejudice, and will therefore be alert to the possible meanings of prejudiced discourses in a group.

Through the expression of prejudice, a group conversation draws a boundary against a despised other. Rather than seeking to 'cure' individuals of prejudice, informal educators seek to counter prejudiced discourses and discriminatory practices. Such prejudiced discourses can be found among professionals as well as among young women and young men, and can be voiced by people of all community backgrounds. It is the power of the discourse, and of the users of it, to marginalise and hurt those it defines as 'other' that needs to be recognised and if possible countered.

Youth workers educate by both 'showing' and 'telling'. A male worker who picks up on apparently sexist remarks in a conversation but is never known to offer to make a cup of tea or wash up is undermining the effectiveness of his educational interventions. Similarly a female worker who pronounces male and female equality but always relies on the male workers to provide the 'security' for the project undermines her own claims.

Most people who express prejudice do so in contradictory ways that could open up to new thinking. It is important to notice whether the prejudices expressed by an individual within a group are also visible in the way in which that individual behaves or whether they are at odds with it. How much of the apparent 'prejudice' is 'groupthink' from which on other occasions individuals are able to show themselves free through their behaviours? Or does the 'groupthink' reinforce individual discriminatory behaviour? How much does it derive from a lack of alternative ways of thinking about the despised 'others' of the prejudiced discourse?

Responding to prejudice and put-downs

Groups of young people can be as full of prejudices, fears and dislikes as groups of adults, and are often considerably less circumspect about expressing them. However, young people are themselves also very likely to be on the receiving end of prejudice. Many staff teams have agreements about always challenging the expression of prejudice and put-downs by young people. There should be an equal commitment to recognising the prejudices which exist within the staff team and to challenge the put-downs and prejudices which are most frequently used against the young people who use the project. In particular it is important to challenge the often class-based prejudice that circulates virtually unnoticed among professionals, such as talk about 'chavs' and 'scallies'.

The prejudices which attach to particular groups are not rational judgements: they often concern sexual behaviour, feelings about dirt and smell, feelings about threat and aggression. They require more than a factual and well-informed response. Responding to prejudice also requires recognition of the non-rational aspects of the prejudice. A practised series of conversational responses enables the educator to signal that a boundary has been crossed yet does not prevent the conversation continuing: 'I'll have to part company with you there when you talk about ....' 'It's not OK to talk about —— here.' Another way of opening a series of challenging conversations is to question the apparent consensus that a prejudiced comment represents: 'You think so? Why do you think that?' Such opening questions can begin a process of probing out of which real dialogue may emerge, over time. It is unlikely that a very deep conversation will happen the instant that this theme emerges. But by questioning and showing, rather than by simply 'telling', the educator can engage an interest which 'telling' will not do. In the challenging conversations about prejudice, the educator's first and repeated strategy is questioning, especially the question *why*? The asking of the question *why* delegitimises prejudice and opens up alternative ways of thinking about the world.

It is sometimes suggested that it is lack of contact with the despised 'others' which fuels prejudice. However, contact alone does not change the reactions or thought patterns on which prejudice is based. For this, the development of counter-discourses is necessary and this is also an important part of the conversations of critical informal education. One common problem which arises in practice is that conversation which focuses on merely correcting prejudicial speech can seem to become a matter of 'guarding your tongue' and 'watching your language' and to be about conforming to a set of externally imposed rules. 'We're not allowed to say that nowadays, are we?' 'It's not PC.' This view is strongly promoted by sections of the press and emerges in jokes about what people are allowed to say. Speech and conversation in this context can be subject to regulation by 'sleeping policemen' or 'traffic cameras'–the talk ranges freely, giving vent to prejudice and hate and is then brought down by the language cop or youth worker. This is the problem which faces the committed practitioner who says: 'Don't let me hear you saying those things in front of me.' If the message is nothing more than 'watch your mouth', it serves only to create distance and suspicion between the professional worker and the young people being challenged. This then makes the process of building trust significantly more difficult.

Rather than engaging in regulatory responses which can easily be experienced as punitive, it is better to make connections with the young people's own experience of being put down and disliked irrationally. 'What does it feel like to be thought of as a "scally" or a "hoodie" just because you live round here?' 'How would you like it if your photograph was being circulated and mocked on the internet?' 'Do you like it when your family is called names?' Youth workers also develop a range of actions which move conversations on so that they do not find themselves stuck in a conversational register of 'admonishing'. They start up opportunities for girls to talk about sex and boys to talk about relationships; they organise rotas based on principles of equality. They bring positive stories and exciting, counter-stereotypical images about the despised groups in to the Youth Centre. This requires a commitment to a relationship with young people, their peer group and their area which will extend over a period of time. Opening up challenges to prejudice and to discriminatory/exclusive practices requires the opening up of conversation over a period of time. This is not a stand-alone six-week programme.

Against put-downs, for self-respect

When there is a sense of envy, or of injustice, or of being 'put down' as a community or neighbourhood, informal educators can begin a process of education in which current injustices facing the community–in relation, for example, to housing or schooling or leisure opportunities–can be made explicit and addressed. The educator can also seek to develop opportunities which celebrate and affirm young people's identities. On a residential, perhaps, some 'time out' away from the ordinary setting, an informal educator will ask: 'What do you like about one another?' and, if trust has built up sufficiently, be amazed at the capacity of young people to reply. 'I'd do anything for my best friend.' This is difficult work as it is often very counter-cultural, especially in communities in which any hint of 'softness' is perceived as dangerous in a world in which both men and women need to be tough to survive. The existence of 'put-downs' as a mechanism for toughening up can be seen as contributing to the self-oppression of members of a poor community and to the likelihood that they will project certain 'victim' qualities, such as weakness or the state of being over-protected and indulgently treated, on to other communities.

Discussion Point

Since many black women were and still are raised in households where most of the love and affection we receive comes from black women elders, mothers, aunts and grandmothers who may also use criticism in a verbally abusive way, we may come to see such practice as a caring gesture and even though it wounds we may imagine the hurting takes place for our own good. (bell hooks, *Sisters of the Yam*, 1993)

What put-downs are used to control young people you are working with?

This experience of being loved but also subject to searing criticism 'for our own good' is by no means limited to Black communities. Many people have been taught that 'self-praise is no virtue'. Conversational practices which encourage different kinds of valuation of our selves in our community are an essential part of the repertoire of youth and community work.

Listening out for: boredom with the limits of the everyday

'Treats', which offer new opportunities and challenge the boredom of the everyday, are another way of expressing a sense of the value of the people the youth worker is working with. Youth and community workers will have up their sleeves opportunities and activities which young people may ordinarily be prohibited from taking part in. Treats characteristically include such 'carrots' as day trips to theme parks; expeditions to take part in relatively more expensive and inaccessible leisure pursuits such as paintballing, roller-blading and ice-skating or bowling–something relatively accessible but sufficiently out of the ordinary and out of the area to require a minibus booking. From this a programme may build up to more demanding activities–adventure activities, cultural activities–that are initially completely outside the frame of reference for a group. This is a valuable response to dissatisfaction with what is on offer on a daily or weekly basis, especially to young people whose families experience poverty and whose lives and opportunities are limited in consequence. The informal educator can give access to the 'spectacular' as well as 'the everyday': residentials; international travel and exchanges; holidays; major arts and music festivals and events–all are part of this element of practice which challenges boredom and finds out the interest in attempting something new.

Key Terms

Conversation that engages young people's interest and moves into new kinds of opportunities and activities is the purposeful conversation of youth work. It is a dialogue which enables information-giving and offers choices about direction and participation to the young person.

Prejudiced discourse and **put-downs** are speech-acts which reinforce inequality and barriers between groups and individuals.

Further Reading

Adams, J. (2007) *Go Girls! Supporting Girls, Emotional Development and Building Self-esteem.* Brighton: TSA.

Allport, G. (1954) *The Nature of Prejudice.* Reading, MA: Addison-Wesley.

Blake, S. and Brown, R. (2007) *Boys' Own: Supporting Self-esteem and Emotional Resourcefulness.* Brighton: TSA.

All of these works explore the impact of prejudiced discourse and of put-downs. The book by G. Allport is the classic starting point for analysing the psychology of prejudice. The other two sources offer examples of practice which challenges the internalisation of such discourses and builds up self-esteem.

Spence, J. and Devanney, C. (2007) *Youth Work: Voices of Practice.* Leicester: National Youth Agency. A research report which offers a rich documentation of the actual everyday practice of youth workers.

Wetherell, M. and Potter, J. (1992) *Mapping the Language of Racism.* Hemel Hempstead: Harvester Wheatsheaf. This text enables the analysis of racist-speech acts as an aspect of wider discourse rather than as an individual 'sick' psychological state.

Part II

Getting to Know Young People
Reflection Points

- What does home mean to the young people you are working with? And what does work mean?
- Do the young people you work with have a sense of 'leisure'? Or the opportunity to travel?
- What meanings do they associate with forming sexual relationships? With having a partner?
- What does parenting mean to the young people you are working with?
- What are the physical, geographical boundaries of your work with young people? What do these boundaries mean?
- How do you work with ground rules in your practice?
- Are any of the groups you work with seen as 'trouble'? Which ones, and why?
- How do you know when someone doesn't want to talk to you and you should disappear? How do you know when they want you around and want you to talk to them?
- Are the young people you work with dissatisfied? Or bored? What with?
- How do you respond to prejudiced talk? Short term? Medium term?
- What was the last positive action you took to support a marginalised group of young people? What was its impact on the conversation?
- What do the young people you work with get excited by?

Part III

Getting Deeper

Safe Space and Identity-based Groupwork

- The establishing and development of closed groups is explained.
- Single-identity groups can offer an important context for learning, but the questions of 'who defines cultures?' and 'who defines identities?' must always be explored.
- The meanings of 'culturally specific practice', 'gender specific practice', 'faith-based practice' and 'work with lesbian, gay, bisexual and transgendered youth groups' are explained.
- The importance of providing contexts in which young people can challenge adult definitions is emphasised.
- The issue of working from identity and 'matching' workers to groups is explored.
- The practice of learning from specific groups can inform the sensitivity to issues of power and identity in all youth work practice.

This chapter presents the case for positive action in relation to identity-based practice. It offers a method of enabling young men and young women to negotiate complex identities. The meanings and purposes associated with the establishment of such work make all the difference.

Culturally specific practice

In a period in which segregation and 'failure to integrate' is seen as a major social problem, the establishment of spaces for culturally specific groups and culturally specific practice is controversial. The work undertaken by Black educators in relation to Black community development forms the basis of 'culturally specific practice' in informal education. Historically, existing youth provision in the UK failed to welcome young men and young women from Black and minority ethnic communities. At the same time, new migrants anxious to retain a close connection with the families and communities they had left behind wished to establish their own community-based provision for their young people. Taken together, this dynamic of exclusion and the response of community-building and self-help led to a pattern of largely separate provision alongside mixed provision in urban centres (Goetschius and Tash, 1967; John, 1981; Williams, 1988).

'Mixing' makes more sense to some migrant communities than others and is facilitated by shared language. Yet language can be a protection to a community as well as barrier to integration. Young people need the opportunity both to mix and to explore their own specific heritage. The 'mother tongue' is important to development for all peoples. Some communities have inherited cultural norms which prevent unsupervised mixing between boys and girls or between people of different faiths. Marriage practices can carry powerful meanings about the future of the people of faith, or of the community, or both. So the reasoning behind 'culturally specific provision' may be based on reasoning which supports traditional definitions of 'community'. It may also create a space in which young people can come together and gain support in questioning traditional assumptions if they wish to do so.

Culturally specific provision should not be seen as substituting for mixed, open and inclusive provision for informal education. Rather, in the tradition of the supplementary schools developed initially by the African-Caribbean communities, it makes a positive addition to or within such provision. Where 'mixed' provision is dominated and led by people from the 'majority' community, or simply where one particular community dominates the provision, 'mixed' provision may make it more difficult to address issues of identity-formation.

In the worst cases, informal educators may be drawn into what have been termed 'colour blind' or 'culture blind' conversations in which the diversity of backgrounds and experiences of young people goes unacknowledged (Chauhan, 1989). A 'colour blind' approach is one in which the approach of youth workers is characterised by the statement: 'We treat everybody the same. We haven't got a problem here' (Gaine, 1995). Problems also occur when the diversity of a group is drawn on primarily for the benefit of (so-called) white participants in a mixed group: an education in urban multi-culture in which the white participants have ready access to the experience of Black and ethnic minority students who become a kind of audio-visual aid for the educator. The conversation of the diverse group then flows in such a way as to be of benefit to the dominant or majority group. The move to provide space for conversations which do not take their agendas from the majority or dominant culture led to the development of 'Black perspectives in youth and community work'. This later became formulated as 'culturally specific work' with young people (Webb, 2001; Chauhan, 2003).

Culturally specific practice aims to enable young people to engage in conversations on their own terms and to their own agendas. Within the boundary of a safe group, young people are enabled to name the issues they seek to negotiate with the wider culture. The term 'minoritised' is used to refer to the experience of groups whose 'minority' status is held to be problematic both for them and for the wider society.

The term 'culturally specific practice' in informal education is a useful way of referring to learning from specific histories, including histories of migration. It can also refer to the conscious learning about the ways in which particular communities have negotiated with a dominant and frequently hostile culture. Culturally specific practice can enable young people to focus on their transition to adulthood very explicitly in relation to their negotiations with their parent/grandparent generation, and in relation to the stereotypes and labels projected on to them by a racist culture. Notions of the extreme patriarchy of Asian cultures or of the aggression of African-Caribbean young men can be investigated and challenged by those most likely to be affected by them and most likely to internalise them. The stereotypes to which a group is subjected become the focus for education as critical enquiry and mutual learning.

This has been particularly important for Asian young women who have been perceived for many years in popular media representations as 'passive' and 'victimised' and now are seen, in their depiction as veil-wearers, as 'passive-aggressive', simultaneously victimised and hostile to the dominant culture. Such stereotypes have a serious impact on all women who are perceived as part of the group 'Asian (Muslim) women' (even if they are Arab in family origin, or Hindu or Christian in their faith) and therefore they are best placed to support one another in developing a response to such stereotypes. The same thing applies to both young men and young women from African-Caribbean heritage communities who are readily perceived as aggressive, whatever their own personal experience of anger. There are many links to be made between the self-help focus of such culturally specific work and a wider political and citizenship education.

The experiences of marginalisation and misrepresentation in the here and now can converge with particularly powerful memories for communities. For example, the history of slavery or empire may seem a long-ago irrelevance to many young people but equally it may seem very personal and relevant and painful to Black and mixed-heritage young people. Young people whose Jewish families faced persecution in the 1930s and 1940s and who migrated to escape persecution will have their own sense of connection with global issues, as will many whose families escaped persecution in later twentieth century, from the Asian families who were expelled from Uganda in the 1970s to Afghan and Iraqi, Somali and Darfuri refugees in the present. The histories and family stories of migration are different again for those whose families came from the Caribbean, from South Asia, from Vietnam or Hong Kong, from Africa or from Latin America, who may still have families 'back home'. Without culturally specific work, it is all too easy for these diverse experiences to be silenced or rendered invisible. In Vipin Chauhan's words,

---

Discussion Point

Culturally specific work enables Black contributions to the development of humanity to be made more specific and visible. It also means that Black perspectives do not only enter informal education in ways which render Black people visible as 'problematic', as exploited or as victims of urban poverty and violence. It means that Black young people can recognise themselves and others as holistic, cultural, spiritual and gifted human beings. (Chauhan (2003) on the Development Education Association and Global Youth Work)

Who defines 'culture'?

The dangers inherent in all 'culturally specific' work are made visible in the thorny question of who defines cultures. 'Who speaks for the community?' is a highly political question (Anthias and Yuval Davis, 1992). Informal education can support young people in investigating what the sources of authority to define a 'culture' or a 'tradition' are. 'Culturally specific practice' is all too often gender blind, just as gender-specific practice is often culture blind. It matters that informal education as mutual learning in these contexts starts with young people's voices that are all too readily marginalised. The concept of 'culturally specific practice' should not be understood as suggesting that tight boundaries can or should be drawn around cultures/communities. Culture is not static or unchanging, and there is a vast ground of common culture in global society, negotiated through the global language of American English. In UK society, in which many young people are at least bilingual, the negotiation of a common culture occurs among a plurality of communities. That the 'common culture' is not the one yearned for by those who are nostalgic for an earlier (and altogether 'whiter') vision of England does not mean that it does not exist, or that it will not change. Specific cultural groups, with specific family patterns and histories of settlement and migration, are in fact continually potentially open to mutual influence in urban multi-culture. The boundaries between groups are always transitioning and changing, and the importance of 'self-identifying' in culturally based work, rather than automatically accepting the labels which have been constructed for us, needs to be emphasised. Cultural networks are historical social constructions, open to development and change as a result of wider patterns of social change.

The points of creativity and development may in fact be found at the edge of communities, among people who make a commitment to the permeability of such borders: through entering into 'mixed' relationships, for example. It is very important that youth workers pay attention to the voices of young people who may feel on the edge of their communities, as these communities are defined by their elders. The question of who has the power to define a community is a very important one. It should always be part of the practice of informal education to question the claims to authority of 'community leaders' who are often older men and to enable new and younger voices to be heard and to create their own definitions of culture and community.

Faith-based practice

Faith-based work can be understood as a development of culturally specific practice in the form of discussions of Islamic youth work, and in the existing traditions of Christian and Jewish youth work. The role of faith-based informal education is not to promote religious teaching: this is the role of the madrasahs, synagogues or Sunday Schools. Faith-based practice is the practice of informal education within the context of self-identifying faith communities.

Muslim youth work, for example, involves a complex set of responses by young people who, in the context of perceived hostility between the West and Islam, identify strongly as Muslim. Muslim young people therefore create a demand for 'Muslim youth work'. The interplay of faith and cultural histories in creating this identification is power-charged. It is best understood as a moment in a chain of conversations, a chain of narrations, which will lead to new definitions of what it means to be Muslim. It enables a legitimation of Islam as one of the faith traditions with which youth work may engage, alongside 'Christian youth work' and 'Jewish youth work'. In the process of establishing itself as a legitimate community of practice, Muslim youth work also creates a potential platform from which 'inter-faith' as well as 'inter-cultural' bridging may happen (Khan, 2006).

The telling and passing on of stories from one generation to another and from one group to another is a very important aspect of culturally specific work, as of all informal education. All the major faith traditions are repositories of stories and memories which keep alive 'dangerous memories' of rebellion and freedom. The role of critical informal education in these faith contexts may well be to enable young people to question their tradition without placing themselves outside its support and embrace.

Gender-specific practice

In the United Kingdom in the nineteenth and early twentieth centuries, during the early period of the development of informal education, the assumption of 'separate spheres' for men and women, for girls' work and boys' work, was very nearly universal. It was based on traditional assumptions about gender-appropriate work. Sewing and raffia work for girls: sport and drill for boys. In the earliest days of youth work, girls' clubs and boys' clubs were separate. Even in those early days, however, there was a feminist influence on practice. Not all of the work was about preparing the boys for military or the girls for domestic service. No less a youth worker than Sylvia Pankhurst, the famous suffragette, makes a brief appearance in the minute books of the Manchester University Settlement, organising a drama club for the girls (Batsleer, 2003). With the success of women's campaign for the vote and recognition of women as equal citizens, this gender segregation began to be challenged, especially the exclusion of women from masculine domains in employment and in education. Non-discrimination in pay and opportunities formed the next successful phase for a politics of women's rights. It may therefore be puzzling that in the late 1970s and 1980s a new generation of feminist activists came to promote gender-specific work, girls' groups from which men were excluded, as a basis for practice which supported women's rights.

The empowerment of women was supported in safe women-only groups from which women might gain confidence to relate to men on more equal terms. The ways in which decisions about the boundaries of a group (in this case the exclusion of men) affected the conversations that occurred was explored. Together young women and women workers could give one another strength and confidence to attempt new things or to name and identify changes that they needed to make in their lives. This may have involved traditionally masculine activities, such as taking leadership roles on climbs or in other more mundane settings. It may have involved attempting simple DIY or vehicle maintenance. It connected to their sense of dissatisfaction with the ways they were treated at work or in their relationships. Discussion in single-sex groups led to campaigns against the use of 'pin-ups' in the workplace as sexually demeaning and eventually led to the development of a vocabulary which enabled the naming of particular patterns of workplace bullying as sexual or racist harassment. Such consciousness-raising discussions also involved naming sexuality and challenging issues of heterosexuality; both the sexual assumptions about masculinity and femininity and the assumption that all girls would eventually grow up heterosexual offered a model of collaborative enquiry into the nature and formation of femininity in conditions of masculine dominance. Furthermore, women practitioners recognised the need to offer adult role models to younger women who were also questioning traditional feminine roles (Carpenter and Young, 1986; Sawbridge and Spence, 1991; Batsleer, 1996).

Initially, this model of practice found it difficult to acknowledge let alone embrace differences between women. When educational and consciousness-raising work begins from a rejection of the stereotypes and assumptions about what it means to be a woman, the inescapable fact that 'women' are not a homogeneous group emerges. It becomes clear that women are historically situated in a variety of ways with complex identities formed by these histories. In relation then to gender, gender-specific work enables young women to investigate together the commonalities and differences in the formation of an adult feminine identity, and to ask the question for themselves which is so often asked of them: 'What do women want?'

This issue of 'difference between women' might apply to obvious differences such as whether or not they are mothers; differences of age; differences of class position. But it may also apply to less obvious differences such as those that lead to liking and disliking, and it relates as much to the desires any of us have for the future as to a shared position in the here and now. When we ask 'What do women want?' the answers may turn out to be much more varied than sex-stereotyping and other 'labels' of either a positive or a negative kind might allow.

The same opportunities to explore the construction of gender also apply to young men working in gender-specific groups, exploring what it might mean to be an adult man or a father. Although exactly the same themes can be explored in mixed groups, the group dynamics change and the investigations are differently inflected. The repertoire of conversation, what it is and is not possible to speak about, changes. Young men will explore the meanings of independence, of being a 'provider', of 'toughness' and 'softness', even of heterosexuality and homosexuality, differently in mixed or gender-specific settings.

Whatever the setting, when working on gender-related themes the educator needs to raise questions about some of the taken-for-granted themes of 'sexual difference'. It is the role of the informal educator to enable the questioning and investigation of what is taken for granted as 'natural' or 'normal'. The inbuilt tendency to define ourselves 'against' the 'other' gender can be either reinforced or investigated in single-sex groups as well as in mixed groups. In gender-specific groups, evidence of some supposedly masculine or feminine qualities belonging to the 'other' gender will be found: men can exhibit so-called 'feminine' qualities of caring to one another; women can make aggression and competitiveness visible, can take risks. Above all, single-gender groups can enable women to explore their own independent 'capacities' rather than accept a 'secondariness' in relation to masculinity. For men, single-gender groups can enable them to explore their needs for care and interdependence without reference to dependence on maternal femininity.

This does not happen automatically however. It is the role of critical informal education to enable this focus, to bring the meanings associated with gender to light, and the presence of the informal educator acts to create safe space, marking the boundary of the group within which such difficult and engaging conversations can safely occur.

Lesbian, gay, bisexual and transgender space

The development of lesbian, gay, bisexual and transgender space has occurred because in most youth and community work there remains a prevailing assumption of heterosexuality. This is sometimes accompanied by an atmosphere hostile to homosexuality, in which homophobia is clearly present and legitimised. In this context, if young people who are lesbian or gay or questioning are to be enabled to explore the meanings of the sexual identity which they are in the process of forming, it is necessary that they have access to a separate, safe space.

Very often these are gendered, with separate spaces made available for gay men and lesbians, but there are also mixed groups which sometimes define the space they are creating as 'queer space'. This may in turn be more hospitable to bisexual people and to transpeople. Such space remains necessary even in a period in which civil partnerships are recognised as weddings and have been rapidly accepted. This acceptance still exists only in a section of the population and cannot be relied upon.

Models of peer support have emerged from the lesbian and gay communities alongside models of mentoring which place great emphasis on the importance of shared experience, shared problem-solving and the potential for mutual learning.

The question of 'matching'

The role of the informal educator in such contexts is to facilitate peer-based conversations. In this context the question of 'matching' emerges, that is the question of the significance of the identity of the worker in facilitating such conversations. To what extent should the youth and community worker facilitating gender-specific, culturally specific or sexuality-specific learning be expected to share the identity of the group with whom he or she is working?

The benefits of working out of a shared sense of identity are enormous. The building up of trust is facilitated as it may be assumed that the worker has shared or at least can imagine from his or her own experience the experiences the young people themselves are investigating and seeking to learn about. A worker who shares to a significant extent the identity of a group of young people with whom she or he is facilitating conversation can offer a role model and is a potential guide. In relation to lesbian, gay and bisexual experience, 'coming out' is strongly supported when a young person has access to a worker who is open about his or her identity and has clearly negotiated and continues to negotiate the coming out process, with him or herself, with his or her family, including parents, with friends and with employers. It shows that what can seem completely impossible during adolescence–acceptance of one's sexuality by those one loves and by the community in which one lives–is in fact possible.

Positive 'role models'?

The concept of 'positive role models' has been an important one in community-based learning, especially when a central focus of the learning is to enable young people to make the transition into their own adult identities successfully. The 'role model' is someone who can be identified with. They offer a template, a model, on which the young person can pattern themselves. This is not the same as copying although it has some elements of copying and repetition. It may also involve the young person observing an adult role model and choosing to do things differently in some subtle ways from them.

This need to act as role models can place an enormous burden on informal educators who are expected to draw on their own complex identities in the course of the work. A role model is not a superhero. When practitioners are acting as role models, they need to learn that they are doomed to disappoint and to learn ways of working through this. Patterns of idealisation and disappointment are complex and need to be understood by staff, as no identification can or indeed should ever be complete. There has to be a process of young people establishing their own independent identity away from the groupwork. Informal education projects which employ staff who share the identities of young people they work with in order to facilitate identity-based work must be fully aware of the supervision and support needs of this group of staff.

'Specific'? 'Sensitive'? 'Safe'?

The fact that there are advantages in seeking some matching of workers should not lead to a situation in which it is assumed that *only* those workers can facilitate culturally specific, gender-specific groups or sexuality-specific groups. It is possible for educators to be *too* well known in a community and for there to be as a result too little space for young people to try out new ways of doing things without feeling they are risking disapproval from community elders. The most important consideration is the skill of the educator in facilitating conversation. It is also vital to recognise that specific spaces can be created for conversation, even where there are not yet staff employed who share the identity of the young people. Working partnerships and diverse teams of staff can enable creative conversations to occur. Co-working between men and women workers, gay–straight co-working and inter-cultural co-working are significant sources of conversational agendas which enable groups to develop in new ways.

One of the most important movements to emerge from the development of identity-based practice has been the peer health, sex and sexuality education movement, and some of the pioneering programmes, such as the 'Beyond Barbie' programme run by the Family Planning Association, were developed by youth workers. It is always important for such education to occur in a safe space. Informal educators are in a position to facilitate choices about enabling sex education programmes to happen in identity-specific groups or in mixed groups in ways that may be less easily available to school-based educators, for example.

Conversations as 'chains of narration'

'Chains of narration', the stories we tell about ourselves and our communities, form connections and change and develop by overlapping, by repetition, but also by incorporating new elements. A tradition, such as separate space for women, interpreted in some settings as confirming women's difference from and subordination to men and confinement in the private domain, may take on a quite different meaning: one that is concerned with 'the dignity of difference' and with 'empowerment'.

Space for the telling of stories from particular faith traditions may become a space for reinterpreting ideas about 'honour' or 'shame'. Sexual practices which previously have been regarded as 'shameful' may be destigmatised through the retelling of stories. In particular this is happening with accounts of homosexuality, which has been stigmatised by the 'Abrahamic' faith traditions but is now being accepted and destigmatised by significant numbers of people within them. This happens in part by the retelling of stories from the faith traditions in ways which affirm rather than stigmatise gay experience. 'Coming out stories' from one generation of evangelical Christian gay men, for example, may give a sense of context and support to the next generation. The dangerous memories of freedom–from slavery, from oppression of a variety of kinds–are kept alive. Such conversations, occurring within boundaried groups, become the 'safe' spaces in which surprises can happen and conversations can take new and very different turns. They enable the old stories to be told with a new inflection, a new set of meanings. This in turn can shift and change the inherited constructed identities and boundaries of the wider society.

It is important to recognise the different meanings of the terms gender-*specific* and gender-*sensitive* work; culturally *specific* and culturally *sensitive* work. All practitioners need to develop such sensitivity, even when not engaged in specific, identity-boundaried practice. This is above all a sensitivity to the ways in which power and identity enter and shape the communities of conversation. It is a sensitivity to the expectations about gender roles, and an openness to facilitating the questioning of them. It is a sensitivity to cultural stories and chains of narration that are available to the young people as well as to the educator taking part in the conversation. It is a sensitivity to the unexpected; unexpected differences and unexpected common ground, in contrast to practice which reinforces stereotyped assumptions, the reified projections of cultural and gender difference which circulate in popular culture. It is a sensitivity which listens carefully for the experiences and understandings which may be silenced in a group and tries out different ways of asking questions in order to bring those experiences to voice. Such sensitivity develops best in teams in which there is a continuing commitment to discussion across difference: to consider the world from the point of view of others and to understand that 'the next question is always more interesting than the last answer'.

Key Terms

Culture as it is used in this context does applies not only to the arts, both popular and elite, but also to the meaning-making practices in which all human beings engage. Cultural boundaries are connected to but not the same as language boundaries and are always changing and porous.

Gender refers to the social construction of sexual difference, to the attributes of masculinity and femininity. As with culture, the meanings (and even the existence!) of gender are always contested.

Further Reading

Chauhan, V. (2003) 'Revolutionising youth work: Black perspectives in global youth work', *Youth and Policy*, 80: 34–44. A useful introduction to global youth work by a key thinker.

Howson, C. and Sallah, M. (2007) *Working with Black Young People*. Lyme Regis: Russell House Press. A collection of essays which shows why identity-based work matters.

Hunt, R. and Jensen, J. (2007) *The School Report: The Experiences of Young Gay People in Britain's Schools*. London: Stonewall.

Khan, M.G. (ed.) (2006) *Youth and Policy,* special issue on *Muslim Youth Work*. This issue presents some of the thinking which has informed the establishment of the Muslim Youth Work Foundation.

The Voluntary Relationship: Competence, Negotiation and Accompaniment

- Voluntary relationship is an essential feature of informal learning; young people learn to negotiate and explore the meaning of competence and consent.
- The idea of 'accompaniment' as a method of youth work which supports young people's growing freedom and autonomy is explained. The meaning of 'respectful relationships' between youth workers and young people is investigated.
- The contribution of the voluntary relationship to the building up of trust is presented.
- The importance and difficulty of trust between individuals and between communities is explored.

Voluntary relationship is fundamental to the practice of informal education. The fact that people choose to take part in youth work rather than being required to do so has been consistently recognised as essential (Davies, 2005). Youth work emphasises the young person's agency as a key feature of professional practice (Spence and Devanney, 2007).

Like children, young people cannot choose whether to go to school until they reach 16 (though some do). In addition, none of us chooses our parents or our siblings. Relationships that we have chosen can enable us to reflect on our patterns of relating with other people and in situations in which we have less choice. The freedom that comes with being able to make choices is one of the characteristics of achieving adulthood. Furthermore, freedom of association, which characterises all informal education, has to be carefully negotiated in work with young people whose lives are subject, as a consequence in part of the very policies which fund the employment of youth workers, to so much scrutiny and surveillance.

Voluntary association has been seen as a characteristic of flourishing democratic societies. Through association, the freedoms of democratic society are developed. This idea of association creating freedom mitigates the rather lonely sense of individual freedom associated with liberal ideas of adulthood as 'autonomy'. It is not only beneficial for individuals but also good for society that citizens engage in education and debate. From the time of the French Revolution onwards, clubs and coffee houses have been places in which dissenting and critical conversations can freely occur. It is not surprising that governments have always sought to regulate such spaces and associations, particularly in times of perceived national emergency. Regulation and surveillance are pervasive in contemporary society and much of what has been termed 'democratic regulation' occurs through the use of personal development measures and in the name of 'personal development'. All this makes it necessary to reconsider the meaning of the 'voluntary relationship' in youth work now.

The transition from child to adult and the increasing ability to consent

Within contemporary constructions of childhood, children are viewed as not able to consent freely and with understanding to the demands, solicitations or offers from others (Archard, 2004). As children grow, so their competence, understanding and capacity to make their own decisions in relationships grows. In addition, young people–during the transition to adulthood–are constructed as having an increasing ability to consent, an increasing agency.

Informal education programmes, including mentoring programmes, have been developed explicitly to explore these transitions to autonomy and autonomous consenting. The negotiation of a voluntary relationship in youth work mirrors the negotiation of consenting relationships throughout life. It is important to learn to say 'yes' or 'no' and to exercise agency about taking part in a youth work programme, partly because it is even more important to be able to exercise choice and consent in the conduct of relationships beyond youth work. This learning about self in relationships was seen as fundamental to 'social education' (what we would now term 'social pedagogy') in youth work from the earliest days of professional training (Gibson and Davies, 1967).

What does it feel like to believe yourself free to say 'yes' or 'no' rather than act in response to the pressures with which you are surrounded? What does it feel like to say 'yes' or 'no' to intimacy and to increasing intimacy in relationships? Conversations prompted by these issues can develop to include themes of abuse, care orders, consent to treatment, criminal responsibility, education, employment, housing, medical treatment and examination, sexual relationships, social security and political participation.

At what age can I ...?

In 2007, the Connexions Service in England published the following brief statement to guide young people and those working with them.

At 13

- You can have a part-time job, with some restrictions

At 14

- You can enter a pub, but you can't buy or drink alcohol there
- A boy can be convicted of rape, assault with the intent to commit rape and unlawful sex with a girl if she is under 16

At 16

- You can have a full time job if you have officially left school. You need to remember that you can't work full time until the last Friday in June–even if you have turned 16 before this.
- You can live independently, subject to certain conditions being met
- You can get married with your parents' or guardians' consent
- You can buy cigarettes and tobacco
- You can ride a moped of up to 50ccs
- You can pilot a glider
- A girl must be 16 before she can legally have sex with a boy
- It is illegal for a boy or man to have sex with a girl under 16, even if she has agreed
- A male may consent to a homosexual act if he and his partner are both over 16
- You can have an abortion without your parents' consent
- A boy can join the armed forces with his parents' or carers' consent
- You can apply for your own passport
- You can have beer or cider whilst eating a meal in a restaurant or an eating area of a pub, but not in the bar

At 17

- You can hold a licence to drive most vehicles
- You can pilot a plane
- You can emigrate
- A care order can no longer be made on you

At 18

- You are legally seen as an adult in the eyes of the law
- You can vote in general and local elections
- You can get married
- You can open a bank account in your name without a parent or carer's signature
- You can buy and drink alcohol in a bar
- You can ask to see your birth certificate if you are adopted
- You can change your name
- You can be called to serve on a jury
- You can sue or be sued
- You can make a will
- You can place a bet
- You can have a tattoo

There are a number of contradictions in these current legal conditions. It seems absurd for example that it is possible to join the armed forces at age 16 but not to vote or to buy an alchoholic drink in a bar. The term 'the age of consent' is commonly used to refer to the age at which the law deems it possible for a young person to enter freely into a sexual relationship: 16 in the UK (with the exception of Northern Ireland, where the age of consent is 17). There is variation internationally, with 14 and 15 being the age of consent in some countries, and with some countries, such as Canada, having a 'near in age' provision in their legal system. There are other significant legal moments–for example, 'the age of criminal responsibility' (age 10 in England and Wales, age 8 in Scotland) which again differs significantly internationally. Other important areas for discussion arise in relation to confidentiality in and consent to medical treatment. Such legal conventions say much about the society's view of child and adolescent development and its stages.

Yet the achievement of adult status legally is not the same as reaching adulthood developmentally. The practice of youth work focuses on the latter, even when the question of 'legal age' is the theme of the conversation. 'The voluntary relationship' which is basic to youth work practice enables and supports the young person's growth in competence and understanding. In the everyday negotiations of activities and opportunities which constitute youth work, issues of consent and agreement are always potentially to the fore. Without the consent and agreement of those involved, nothing can happen. Informal educators have to win consent. Youth workers work with young people who want to work with them, rather than with young people who have to be there. Even when they work as informal educators in schools or prisons or Youth Offending Teams, the consent of the young people to taking part in the relationship and the conversation makes the difference. Just as the freedom of the citizen can best be measured in the existence of opportunities to practise dissent in a society, so the voluntary nature of the relationship created in youth and community work must be grounded in the 'freedom to walk away' or, at the very least, the freedom to opt out.

A classic definition of freedom is found in John Stuart Mill's *On Liberty*:

> the only purpose for which power can be rightfully exercised over any member of a civilised community against his will is to prevent harm to others. His own good, either physical or moral, is not a sufficient warrant.

Such a view of the freedom of the participants in informal education makes it impossible to compel them to take part in a project which the educator thinks will be good for them, which might even objectively be recognised as 'good for them'. Their participation cannot be compelled, only enticed.

Learning through voluntary relationship: the accompaniment model

So it is through the voluntary relationship with young people that youth work supports personal development. Conversation which supports young people's growth into autonomy and freedom has been called 'accompaniment'. The idea of accompaniment is particularly valuable in relationships with individuals, including guidance and mentoring relationships, but is not exclusive to them. The metaphor of accompaniment has its roots in music, in the relationship between a soloist and accompanist undertaking a performance together. It conveys something of the quality of listening and attention which the informal educator gives, not taking centre stage but working responsively with the main performer, keeping time and stopping with them. The social script which is both created and followed by the informal educator and young person is not fixed and marked in the fashion of a musical score. The metaphor is more accurately a metaphor of improvisation on a chosen theme, the accompanist following the player. Conversations go off at tangents, take new turns, new topics are introduced.

The image of music and accompanist suggests a level of co-operation without requiring equality. The relationship between the players, as between the youth worker and young people, is not a relationship of equality. It is nevertheless a relationship of co-operation in a shared purpose, a relationship of mutuality and respect. As in the relationship between players performing together, there are distinct parts to be performed, and at different moments different balances are found between the players. There will be times when the rhythms of the conversation move in unison. At other times, the conversation will develop through a pattern of dominance and subordination and the voices of those involved will be shifting out of balance or seeking a new balance. The youth worker, simply as a consequence of being more mature than the young people they are accompanying, will have the most powerful voice and already established views on many matters. At some points, these views and their voice will dominate the conversation. But more often, in order to create balance and mutuality in the conversation, the youth worker will need to practise reserve in order to let the other voices through fully to play their part.

The metaphor of accompaniment also holds the sense of providing companionship on a journey. The one who accompanies, the youth worker, needs to be prepared for the journey. Yet the journey is the young person's, uniquely. This means being prepared to act as a support in places, at times and in ways that may take the youth worker out of their comfort zone: it is the young person's own journey of discovery. This particular conversation has never happened before. However, even in the case of very intimate or painful conversation, the youth worker, the one who accompanies, may have had conversations *like this* before. The young people have never made their transition from childhood to adulthood before, have never had the conversations of their own transition before and will never have them again. Accompanying involves some familiarity with the landmarks of the journey from childhood to adulthood but also requires recognition that each conversation is a new conversation. In some accounts, accompaniment is a spiritual or humanistic practice: one concerned not with this or that aspect of transition (education, or employment or training, or sexual relationships for example) but with the whole. That whole is concerned with the exploration and investigation of what it means to be human (Green and Christian, 1998).

Non-violence in the practice of accompaniment

When young people are separating from particularly strict boundaries established in childhood, they sometimes 'go wild' in a variety of ways, finding it impossible to establish boundaries of safety for themselves. Safety is important. Young people are reassured by practitioners who take certain basic measures of safety. These include not working in isolation, working in teams, using mobile phones issued from work and direct contact with a line manager/supervisor in case of emergencies.

Once such non-negotiable conditions for working are established, contracts and ways of working may be established more or less formally, created in dialogue with the participants, and reinterpreted and revisited as people come and go from groups and conversations. They will include expectations about respecting and not judging, about confidentiality and gossip, and about openness to change. The notion of relationships as respectful and trusting is one that is of special significance.

Understanding of these conditions for conversation changes and develops. Sometimes informal educators have important information to share or warnings to give about the circumstances a young person is in and the choices they are facing. Such speech is like a 'Danger!' road sign, containing an active warning as well as a message: 'Don't go there.' Sometimes the youth worker can bring an experience to voice, such as delight, or joy, or anger, or uncertainty or encouragement. Interruptions become part of the flow of the conversation. Interruptions are born of excitement, engagement, anxiety, non-rational passions of various kinds. The places and times of youth work can be places and times for trying out new ideas and new scripts, without fear of being harshly condemned or looking impossibly foolish or uncool. Much more often than speaking, however, the informal educator is involved in listening, listening others into speech, listening without interrupting

Respectful conversations

'Respect.' 'Don't judge.' Thinking about what it means to treat one another with respect always raises the question of passing judgement. We are often rightly afraid of the judgement of others, of mutual appraisal and assessment.

The discourse of respect offers a sense of mutuality and recognition, but it also has the opposite meanings. Its reference to codes of hierarchy and power has not been lost: in street culture 'respect due' may be a demand for payment to a gang leader or a demand for revenge; in politics it may mean either conforming to community-led expectations about noise, rubbish and the use of public space or else seeking punishment for those who do not conform.

In youth work, respect needs to be a two-way exchange. It is 'mutual respect' which is needed. So the meaning of the term 'respect' needs to be investigated in each new conversation. Historically, respect was owed by social inferiors to social superiors, but not the other way round. Now, however, the question of what it might mean for the socially more powerful to respect those with less power needs to be asked and answered. It does not mean going along with everything a young person says or does, just because they are young.

Some groups of young people develop practices associated with 'being of value' and the building up of 'respect' and status within a group which are very much at odds with the values of the youth project. This seems to make 'mutual respect' difficult. The informal educator/youth worker may be judged according to street codes and values and found wanting. At minimum, they are seen as lacking in any style sense. In turn, the youth workers may judge the practices of drug use, of sexual relating, of theft by the young people as 'wanting'. Such mutual critical appraisals can mean that a sharply judgmental and assessing tone comes to dominate the conversations: trust does not develop and the safe space that is needed for developmental work is not created. If what gives status and the codes of ethics that are operating are very much in conflict, mutual respect can prove very difficult to achieve.

Each person has, however inarticulately, a sense of the practices and meanings which give them, in their own lives, a sense of worth. Some young people and adults have strong investment in finding a sense of worth in practices that are self-destructive. Without necessarily being fully conscious of it, they assign high value and status to, for example, taking and driving cars at speed, or starving themselves into smaller and smaller fashion sizes, or other risky behaviour. If other people engage in these practices too, a sense of mutual respect is generated, even when the overall practice is self- and other-destructive.

There is therefore a need to move the basis of 'respect' away from codes of honour, and the recognition and assessment of behaviours against a hierarchy of 'correctness' or 'worth' to some other basis. 'Respect' could be defined as regard for the being and becoming of another person, even when there is no acceptance of the codes of honour by which they operate.

If youth and community workers find this basic stance impossible–perhaps because of the political affiliations of particular groups or because of a fundamental breach of the conditions of non-violence–then the youth and community workers need to be supported to withdraw from the conversation. But taking the risk that such a stance *is* possible has been the basis of much creative and courageous practice.

Confidentiality and openness

The part played by a trusted adult is recognised over and over again in accounts by young people of what makes a difference to their experience of youth work and youth activities. It is not activities alone that support young people, not just, in the words of current policy, 'things to do and places to go' but above all 'people to talk to, people to be with'. The role of the youth worker as a trusted adult should never be minimised.

Confidentiality needs to be stated explicitly. 'This will go not further.' The informal setting can lead young people to assume that what they share in conversation with one another or with a worker will go no further, but this cannot be taken for granted.

There are two specific situations in which confidentiality cannot be guaranteed. The first is where a young person is disclosing information which leads the worker to believe that they and or another child are in danger of violence or abuse. This must be reported to the person responsible for child protection within the team. The second is a situation in which the worker is in a partnership–for example with the Connexions service or with a Youth Offending Team–which is concerned with tracking the movements of particular young people, including for example young care leavers and young people at risk of re-offending. It is a fundamental breach of the practice of informed consent to undertake such 'tracking' covertly.

It is then possible for the worker to maintain an agreement about confidentiality in practice and about how and to whom the content of the conversations is represented. In relation to decisions affecting health and well-being for example, there is clearly a balance to be struck between interventions which seek to protect a child and interventions which respect the growing autonomy of young people able to make competent decisions about their own health and well-being. On this reasoned basis, conversations about illegal or under-age drug or alcohol use can be protected by confidentiality.

Since informal education conversations often occur in groups as well as in one-to-one contexts, youth workers need to draw attention to issues of safety in groups and the ways in which the boundaries of confidentiality may be breached by group members. For example, the sharing of confidences about sexual practice within an 'unsafe' group can lead to the development of a reputation for sexual availability which may circulate within wider networks and then become the source of further intensified vulnerability. The conversational strategies of the educator need to be such as to protect young people from sharing personal information too freely at the beginning. Sensitive topics can be explored and investigated by the educator bringing resources to a session which enable pertinent and relevant topics to be explored without provoking unsafe disclosures or risking rumour.

A basic stance of openness is necessary. As with all education, there is a commitment to following the conversation wherever it may lead, to enabling greater expectations to be voiced, minds to be changed. This openness is–as much as confidentiality–the basis from which trusting relationships can develop and grow. For conversations to be able to support development, there has to be both openness and responsible risk-taking. There will necessarily be failures, wrong turnings, mistakes made. The capacity of youth work to enable learning and development lies in the ability to enable young people to take risks and to identify and overcome fear of failure.

Trust

The fact that relationships are voluntary and freely entered into is an essential basis for negotiating trusting relationships of accompaniment.

Inherited power dynamics of gender, culture and class and the negotiation of difference can all make building trust more difficult. Trusting relationships are ones in which those involved have entered into a commitment for the future, however time limited that future may be, and reliability and trustworthiness in keeping those commitments is an essential feature of making and keeping safe spaces.

Trust in the respectful relationships established by youth workers enables young people to show themselves ignorant, weak and vulnerable and therefore open to change and open to learning. Such trust militates against people becoming discouraged or resentful in the face of unequal capacities within a group, and encourages the valuing of different kinds of talent and capability. Some people have visual intelligence, some are verbal, and some are good with numbers, others good with how things work, others musical or academic. All these capabilities can be encouraged within trusting groups even when society as a whole is based on the rewarding of certain kinds of merit and talent over others. However, establishing trusting relationships which encourage learning, development and change is a challenging task in the context of power relationships of gender, cultural diversity and class.

Community-based projects which offer informal education opportunities to everyone, of all ages in the community, and not just to the young, make an enormous difference. Such methods might offer more hope and respect to communities than the implementation of dispersal orders can. Some of these methods are explored in the final chapter of this book.

This chapter has explored the meanings of young people's freedom and increasing competence to consent as a basis of youth work conversations. It has further explored what is meant by 'accompaniment' and 'respectful conversation,' with a particular emphasis on the process of building trusting relationships. The scale of the task of creating trust in a political culture in which trust has been eroded cannot be underestimated. This breakdown of trust, and the consequent emphasis on 'homeland security' and other forms of security is creating the context for youth work. This makes the antagonism between methods of youth work based on the 'voluntary relationship' and responses to young people based on surveillance and control increasingly evident.

Key Terms

Voluntary relationship has been taken as a critical indicator that youth work is possible. It should not be confused with the issue of setting (youth work can and does take place in schools, for example) but the fact that informal learning happens in times and places that participants are 'free' in matters. In a voluntary relationship, all participants are free to exercise agency and choice.

Confidentiality as a basis for support and information-giving is highly prized and only to be questioned when there are issues of child protection to be considered. Confidentiality, along with informed consent, offers safe space to young people when they need privacy. However, informal learning is an **open space of enquiry**, and therefore not mainly conducted in highly confidential spaces.

Further Reading

Colley, H. (2003) *Mentoring for Social Inclusion: A Critical Approach to Nurturing Mentor Relationships*. London: RoutledgeFalmer. This book provides a rich discussion and critique of the rhetoric of mentoring, the limitations and possibilities of mentoring as a practice, and has a good chapter on better practices.

Davies, B. (2005) *Youth Work: A Manifesto for Our Times*. Leicester: National Youth Agency. This provides a clear short account of why the voluntary relationship matters so much.

Sennett, R. (2003) *Respect in a World of Inequality*. New York: Norton. This book is the basis for the discussion of respect in this chapter.

11

Friendship and Professionalism

- The dilemmas of 'friendship' as an aspect of informal learning in youth work are explored.
- Boundaries, closeness and distance in professional practice are explored.
- The practice of friendship as a practice of hospitality, generosity and welcome in a network of learning is discussed.

One of the most notable features of the contact between the professional informal educator and those with whom she or he is working is its friendliness. Because of the informality of the work, the ways in which youth and community workers establish their relationships with young people and adults are much less distinctly distant than the style adopted by other professionals, such as teachers and health workers. Yet the view of the informal educator as a 'friend' is contentious. The more the professional identity of informal educator has developed, the less easy it seems to hold on to the notion of the youth and community worker as 'guide, philosopher and friend'.

The notion of friendship has been significant from the start, in the role played by middle-class pioneers in the University Settlements promoting friendship as a bond between classes. In the 1930s, Basil Henriques, the Warden of Baron St George's Jewish Settlement in the East End of London, argued that it was important that the head of a boy's club get to know and understand really well every individual member. 'He must have it felt that he is their friend and their servant' (Smith and Smith, 2002). Not, it must be noted, that he must *be* their friend or their servant. Rather, that they must feel him to be so. The ideal of service, embracing as it did a construction of the role of the youth worker as an *ally* to the boys, emerged strongly from a Christian ethic. In 2005, a worker in a Lesbian, Gay, Bisexual Support Project was asked by one of the young people with whom she was working if she would go out with him as it was his birthday and he had no friends with whom to celebrate. She explained that she was unable to do so as she was his worker rather than his friend. Instead she arranged a birthday celebration for him at the project. The ethos of professionalism led her explicitly to deny that she was his 'friend', yet in fact she continued to act in a spirit of friendship towards him.

Between these two moments stand the years in which the public services–of education and welfare–became professionalised and in the process gained secure salaries, status and recognition and lost some of the sense of themselves as a vocation or calling.

Profession vs calling

Mark Smith and Michelle Smith have suggested the following terms of comparisons between the discourses of friendship and professionalism.

delivery (for professionalism) as distinct from being (for calling);
client as distinct from friend/member;
boundary as distinct from relationship;
manage as distinct from organise;
intervention as distinct from conversation;
outcome as distinct from learning;
evaluation as distinct from reflection;
and procedure as distinct from judgement. (Smith and Smith, 2002)

The binary model helpfully clarifies a number of tensions. The cost is to disguise the overlap between the two positions and to silence some aspects which are not polarised. There is more than a suggestion here that 'professionalism' inevitably leads to a reduction of all that is educationally important to what can be measured, managed, counted, assessed and improved. Since informal education has historically existed in tension with such utilitarian approaches to schooling, Smith and Smith imply that the language of 'vocation' is more fitting to the work.

Yet everything that is named in the grouping under 'calling' could equally be found under the term 'professional', if the term professional is re-interpreted in terms of autonomy. Informal education professionals can and should spend time being alongside club or project members; form relationships with them; engage in learning through conversation; support young people in the organisation of activities. To become professional does not necessarily imply such a loss of spirit.

There is a persistent fear that the 'spirit' or 'values' or 'ethos' of youth and community work may be endangered. On the whole they are seen as most endangered by government initiatives which seek to bind and control the direction of the work. Curiously, 'professionalisation' and accountability seems to imply a loss of autonomy, whereas, historically, to be professional was precisely to be accountable to a professional code of ethics rather than to the Government's policy agenda or to commercial targets. The shift of meaning is an indication of the extent of the erosion of trust and belief in 'professional culture', and the real loss of autonomy, during the late twentieth century.

Smith and Smith suggest that the emphasis of professionalism is on technique as distinct from ethics, practical wisdom and the desire to act truly and rightly. It is however possible to re-imagine the youth and community worker as 'guide, philosopher and friend', without thereby abandoning the ground gained in the professionalisation of informal education and public services. The ground gained has served the 'profession' well in terms of pay and conditions of employment, and has served young people well in terms of providing staff and support whose presence can be relied on.

Professionalisation

The creation of the modern professions of nursing, school teaching, social work and youth and community work coincided with the growing necessity for a secure and independent income for the unmarried women who developed such work in the first half of the twentieth century. In the second half of the century, as the work became securely professionalised, it first opened up to men and then became dominated by them in the senior positions. The investment in rank and status and minute distinctions of office and 'line management' became very marked. (There were three different professional associations in the Youth Service, depending on the status of staff.) At the beginning of the twenty-first century the picture is different again, with the profession being female-dominated and with men and women reasonably equally represented in senior positions.

The development of a 'profession' strengthened the capacity of local authorities to offer a consistent service to young people and youth organisations in their localities. Specific skills, knowledge and abilities were held to be necessary in the development of the work, and these skills, knowledge and abilities required education, training and a specific professional formation, distinct from or certainly in addition to that offered to teachers or social workers. 'Professionalisation' has enabled the development of a community of practice with an academic and professional literature to support it.

Professionalisation has also secured a set of standards for practice which it would have been very difficult to develop outside such a framework. Furthermore, in the context of faith-based practice, there are limitations to the idea of 'calling' which need to be attended to carefully. The idea of calling, with its undoubtedly faith-based and religious underpinnings, can seriously limit the degree of accountability of a practitioner in an unacceptable way. It is possible for a practitioner to believe that he or she has been placed outside ordinary frameworks of accountability and to be 'accountable only to God and to their calling'. This can enable dangerous practice to develop unchecked. 'Friendship' describes a very important aspect of youth working but this need not undermine a commitment to professionalism.

Friendship as usefulness, friendship as pleasure, friendship as pursuit of the good

Contemporary philosophical writing on friendship starts from Aristotle's classical definitions, which in some ways simply enable us to distinguish friends from enemies: friendship as usefulness, friendship as pleasure and friendship as mutual pursuit of the good. In these terms, many relationships of education might be termed friendships.

The notion of the informal educator as useful friend, one who produces and provides 'really useful knowledge', is an idea of long standing, found from the earliest days of modern informal education in the work of Friendly Societies and mutual improvement societies. 'Really useful knowledge' was a term used by educational radicals in the nineteenth century to refer to knowledge about social conditions, in a direct contrast to the knowledge promoted by the Society for the Promotion of Useful Knowledge, which promoted literacy only in order to support the reading of the Scriptures. 'Really Useful Knowledge' in contrast promoted literacy in order to offer explanations of why injustice flourished and of what led people to experience the conditions of life that limited and oppressed them (Cohen, 1990). In this sense, the early clubs and institutes were 'friends educating each other'.

Friendship as pleasure suggests that enjoyment and mutual delight in the work characterise informal education at its best. Without pleasure and enjoyment and enough mutual liking, it is hard to imagine youth work becoming established. Clubs and associations dedicated to particular leisure pursuits are a significant aspect of civil society. For the informal educator such 'organising around enthusiasms' in a neighbourhood or district is an invaluable resource. People's pleasure in their hobbies and their willingness to share this pleasure across the generations provides both a model and an inspiration for young people in the pleasures to be found pursuing an interest for its own sake and in the mutuality to be found in clubs and associations throughout life.

The third aspect of the classical definition of friendship–friendship as the mutual pursuit of the good–needs further interrogation. Smith and Smith argue that all involved in education need to be friends of truth. In a world of competing claims to truthfulness, it is surely the case that being 'a friend of truth' means making these competing claims visible, and recognising the polyvalency of truth rather than passionately defending one truth alone. Discussion about what truth or goodness is or where it can be found happens constantly, because of the nature of our understanding of truth in the contemporary world. The existence of such discussions and debates also offers a reality check for the youth worker's claims about 'voluntary association' and conversation. It is all too easy for the educator to assume that they have a monopoly on truth.

Friendship in contemporary culture

There is a large gap between this classical account of friendship and more privatised understandings of friendship which permeate contemporary culture. The problems associated with seeing the youth and community worker as a friend, as one who desires the good of the other, do not derive from the classical model but from the contemporary context, in which there is a strong privatisation of the idea of 'friendship'. It is highly particularistic, suggesting preference and exclusivity. While it may be possible to attempt to love everyone, even one's enemies, it is not usually seen as possible or desirable in contemporary terms to attempt to be everyone's friend. In fact, someone who is 'everyone's friend' may be deemed untrustworthy and open to suspicion.

Friendship in modern terms is often, though not only, a dyadic relationship, a pairing. This, on its own, is too exclusive a pattern for the conversations of informal education which are characteristically more associational and network based, aiming perhaps to create a 'group of friends'. There is clearly an important place for 'one to one conversations' but they need to be rooted in 'a group of friends' or a club, or in the virtual spaces of discussion lists, noticeboards and chat rooms, which provide the contemporary equivalents of the 'friends educating one another' of the Victorian mutual improvement societies, with many opportunities for finding companionship and fellowship there.

Professional boundaries

Some informal education conversations are one to one: for example conversations which occur as part of mentoring relationships or in street work and befriending projects. It may be here that there is most scope for confusion. Some of the language in which friendship has been described–'reciprocity; mutual possession; mutual self-abandon'–can sound very like the language of relationship between lovers. There are degrees of friendship, degrees of closeness and, importantly, limitations on mutuality between those involved with one another in a professional capacity, or involved with one another as educators. Recognising when and how those relationships shift, and finding the level and degree of mutuality that is appropriate, is very important in the creation of safe spaces. It is in the confusion of roles and in particular in the confusions about power in relationships that the potential for harmful abuse in the context of informal education lies.

Whilst it should go without saying that sexual relationships between youth workers and young people are to be avoided, there is also the issue of what happens when someone 'falls in love' with an educator. Very often this can happen in relation to an investment by a young person in a powerful figure, an authority figure. A young person who experiences a great lack of closeness or comfort or parental affection imagines in their relationship with a worker the possibility of meeting some of those needs. Recognising and finding ways of dealing with such projections is important and supervision is the space in which they can best be addressed.

Sometimes the idea of a 'calling' can further invest the worker with an aura of 'charismatic' authority. The confusion between the idea of closeness to God, even to the love of God, and the love of a particular leader who couches their work in terms of 'faith ministry' is not uncommon. It is for this reason that many churches and faith organisations have developed rigorous and rule-based child protection procedures. However, when these procedures are not well understood they can appear to be designed more to protect individual staff from allegations than to really promote understanding of the complex issues of power in professional relationships, in which context both safe and loving relationships and the abuse of love and trust can occur.

The negotiation of personal boundaries and limits is not only a professional concern. The negotiation of boundaries concerns the ways in which people are able to relate to one another, to relations between 'self' and 'other', to separation and connectedness. Such boundaries are present all the time and are constantly having to be recognised and respected or negotiated and changed. Boundaries are negotiated in leisure space, workplace relationships, personal friendships and intimate relationships between lovers. That is to say, the process of creating boundaries, changing them, recognising them, making mistakes about them and so on does not only happen in relation to intimacy. As relationships develop, and depending on the degree of closeness, boundaries change and shift. It is this which is at stake when 'boundaries' are discussed in informal education.

What is needed is an understanding of the ethics of closeness, and an understanding of the presence of the practitioner as creating a professional boundary for safe space in which learning can occur. This boundary—which is breached by sexual contact and by violence—is necessary to the establishment of a learning relationship in which the development of the young person remains paramount.

Any discussion of the ethics of relationships between practitioners and young people must be based on an understanding of the professional power of the youth and community worker and the responsibilities of care which an adult owes to a young person. Adult/child power dynamics are caught within a matrix of power, in which many aspects of identity, particularly perhaps in this context dynamics of gender and sexuality, create the context for developing ethical practice. If a closeness is developing between an adult and a young person which might lead to an abuse of power, this needs to be explored and discussed in supervision. It may mean that the relationship is developing primarily for the benefit of the worker rather than out of a mutual 'friendship for the network of learning' or out of a primary commitment to support for and development of the young person.

No amount of discussion of vocation or calling should take attention away from the importance of safe boundaries which protect a young person from taking on an adult role too rapidly in relation to the personal support of practitioners. The best way of preventing this is by regular supervision which includes space for staff to explore the emotional aspects of their work.

The issue of mutuality in friendship is not only an issue in the context of sexual feelings and their expression. If a member of staff is relying on closeness to young people to meet their own emotional needs, this needs to be explored in supervision, as it can have a significant impact. Sometimes, however, close relationships between workers and a few young people can enhance the development of informal learning for a much wider group. This issue has been well understood in religious communities for many centuries. Monastic traditions warned against 'particular friendships' on the grounds that they place a limitation on the love that can be expressed within a community. This is another way of saying it is best to try to avoid having favourites! However, working with a few people closely, in order to expand the horizons and expectations of a wider group, is an important element of practice. How all this is negotiated is not merely a matter of procedure, but a profoundly ethical question, and this too needs the support of skilled supervision. Boundaries which enable safe space for valuable and valued conversation also protect the professional practice of friendship within a group, network or community.

Local workers and local friendships

It is absolutely necessary—if the sense of informal learning as 'friends educating each other' is to have any meaning—that informal education has room for reciprocity and mutual give and take. In particular it must have room for the educator to be educated in the realities in which the people she or he is working with live their lives. The difficulties as well as the strengths of informal educators being drawn from their own local communities, and attaining professional qualification to practise through their work in those communities deserve careful exploration. Practitioners who are drawn from 'inside' particular communities have a range of resources and practices at their disposal for making immediate connections, rapidly making a reading of the issues faced in those communities and building up dialogue. 'Insiders' have often been recognised and valued as gatekeepers to particular communities, enabling conversations to occur across boundaries and sometimes giving access to the communities to professionals with agendas that come from elsewhere. The 'locals', the 'indigenous workers', are undoubtedly necessary to the nationals and the 'globals'.

After the riots in London, Liverpool, Manchester and Leeds in the early 1980s, there were various attempts to engage the youth of those areas through the development of schemes such as apprenticeship schemes for youth and community workers. This involved a recognition that people from those areas tended not to be present in educational and training courses after the end of compulsory schooling. It also involved a recognition that the 'quietening' of the discontents of those communities was most likely to happen as a result of involving local people in the process. The apprenticeship schemes for youth and community workers represented a commitment to offering qualifications to practitioners from specific urban areas. This can be understood in terms of community development as a form of cultural imperialism, an inheritance from the practices of the colonial period. Equally, and in contrast, it has been seen and experienced as a method of affirming local voices and knowledge, against centralised and bureaucratic knowledge.

For practitioners who are insiders, however, particularly those who live and work in the same community, it can mean that they are never 'off the job'. Being both an 'insider' and a professional raises issues of trust, safety and confidentiality in acute ways. Can young people ever be completely confident that what they are discussing will not get back to their parents via the workers? There is sometimes a belief that workers from one's own community are less professional and that informal educators will feel more accountability to their own 'community networks' than to the young person they are working with. This poses challenges for the practitioners who work in their own community: to establish a sense of friendship, trustworthiness and reliability in not breaking confidences and unequivocally 'being there' for the young people they are working with. To be an outsider however does not necessarily mean to be neutral or to be more capable of disinterested friendship. Issues of trust and ethics are also there for outsiders: how will they treat what they learn about this neighbourhood, about what matters here? Where will their loyalties lie? Can they demonstrate themselves to be an allies and friends to the community, to the young people? Can hard, challenging things said in friendship be accepted from them, as outsiders? It is in recognising and crossing such boundaries that change happens through the practice of youth and community work.

The practice of friendship in a network of learning: friendship, generosity and openness

The practice of friendship (according to all the world's faith traditions) is a practice of hospitality and generosity. To be a friend is to be welcoming, generous, to be hospitable, to stand with an open hand. This is the stance from which informal education as a practice of friendship must begin. Talking about boundaries and limits can sound inimical to such openness.

The hospitality and generosity encouraged by many faith communities constantly asks questions not about the existence of boundaries but about how and where the boundaries are drawn. From a faith perspective, boundaries tend to be drawn with too much of an eye to self-protection and the drawing of limits, and with considerable scope for an increase of generosity, openness and accessibility. Who and what is excluded from conversations because they occur between 9 a.m. and 5 p.m., because they do not happen at weekends, because they happen in places where girls go and not boys, or vice versa, because they happen in places where this community goes but not that other one? In a discourse of friendship which is about generosity and openness the concern for boundaries will always lead to questions about inclusion and exclusion. Exactly who and what possibilities are being excluded when boundaries and limits are drawn in the way that they are?

Practices of friendship rooted in traditions of hospitality and generosity cannot evade close questioning themselves about what they enable and what they limit. They need to engage with the power implicit in the position of the giver and the potential victimisation implicit in the position of one who receives, the passivity and vulnerability associated with being on the receiving end of a gift. 'Doing good to others' can be a highly persecutory practice. To have good done to you can be a terrifying ordeal, if you have had no say in what the definition of 'good' is. 'She was a woman who went about doing good to others. You could tell the others by their hunted look,' C.S. Lewis famously remarked. It is from a recognition of these power dynamics that the expression 'cold as charity' comes. The following case study highlights some possibilities and pitfalls in seeking to 'span the world with friendship', or at least extend its scope.

Case Study

Disabled people and their allies: an example of some pitfalls and possibilities of friendship

In 1957, the National Association of Youth Clubs set up the PHAB clubs. At the time, disabled young people's lives were largely lived out in completely segregated settings and their opportunities for schooling and education, as well as leisure and recreation, were highly restricted. The PHAB clubs–Physically Handicapped and Able-bodied clubs–were an attempt to create new opportunities for disabled young people and to break down their segregation from the wider society. The able-bodied young people who became involved with the clubs, like many who are drawn to work on the issue of disability today, were perceived as motivated by a kind of paternalistic benevolence and a desire to 'do good'. Little is known of the actual motivations of able-bodied members who became involved with PHAB, but by the 1970s such initiatives were being strongly criticised as inhibiting rather than promoting change by the emerging disabled people's movement. Under the slogan, 'Rights not charity' disabled people engaged in a series of demonstrations and direct actions which successfully highlighted the problem of the representation of disabled people as the objects of welfare and charitable interventions rather than subjects of their own lives.

Television-based charities such as the Telethon and Comic Relief were confronted for their representation of disabled people as 'needy victims' or as 'brave and tragic heroes'. Young disabled people could no longer be viewed as appropriate objects for other young people's volunteering activities. This political movement eventually led to the enactment of the Disability Discrimination Act and the Special Educational Needs Discrimination Act and the establishment of the Disability Rights Commission, now formally part of the Human Rights Commission.

However, the identity politics of the disabled people's movement and the establishment of informal education and youth work which was truly integrated (on young disabled people's terms) and/or which offered real scope to the development and autonomy of young disabled people required from the very beginning a sense of coalition, and a sense of what it means to 'act in friendship'. Once the medical definitions of specific impairments had been superseded in youth work by discussions of a social model which required that attention be paid to the barriers imposed by the social and physical arrangements of projects, the need for a practice of advocacy and self-advocacy became clear.

The role of carers, family members and volunteers came under intense scrutiny. Non-disabled people were drawn into the movement, but not this time as people undertaking negatively defined 'charity work'. They were seen as 'allies' and 'friends' to the movement, and in acting as friends and allies their role was very closely monitored and directed by the disabled people who were spearheading the movement. Friendship to a practice of learning, and professional friendship to disabled people turned out to involve a great deal of letting go of assumptions and unlearning of old and supposedly helpful habits on the part of able-bodied practitioners.

The role of 'friends' and 'allies', as highlighted by the disabled people's movement, is never to speak for young people instead of them speaking for themselves. When youth workers act as friends, they may advocate but only in terms decided by the young person. It is not the youth worker's role to represent 'the best interests' of the young person, but rather to enter into honest dialogue to help them clarify and voice their own perspective, and to use such power as they have at their disposal to strengthen this voice. This is what friends and allies do.

This chapter has explored some of the current debates about youth and community work as 'friendship'. In so doing, it has explored further the issue of professional boundaries and how they are used to create safe space for work with young people. It has taken the idea of friendship beyond the question of what happens in 'one to one' conversations and has explored the role of the youth and community worker in relation to closeness and distance, insider or outsider, participant or ally in the struggles of young people in their neighbourhoods or communities of interest.

Key Terms

Allies. The term, allies, as it is used in the context of the disabled people's movement, extends the thinking about friendship in order to embrace a political sense of creating support for a set of demands for change.

Further Reading

Davies, B. (1999) *A History of the Youth Service in England Vol. 1 1939–1979. From Voluntaryism to Welfare*. Leicester: Youth Work Press. This explores some of the history and prehistory of professionalism in youth and community work.

Young, Kerry (2006) *The Art of Youth Work*. Lyme Regis: Russell House. This offers a much more critical discussion of friendship and professionalism.

Animation, Informal Education and Creativity

- Informal learning is understood as a practice of animation.
- Play and imagination are essential underpinnings of informal learning as animation.
- Arts-based informal learning enables access to important sources of creativity throughout adolescence and adult life: examples of practice come from theatre, dance, music and from the visual arts.
- Creativity draws on both active and passive aspects of the self. The contemporary climate in education values activity over passivity and the disciplines of waiting and non-effort. There is a danger that, in this climate, creativity in youth work will be lost.

Case Study

Some youth workers took a group of young people from the city on a camping trip in a rural area. At the beginning of the week, one of the young men robbed the charity box in the fish and chip shop. There was trouble. It provided some excitement. At the end of the weekend, they found themselves suddenly playing a game of hide-and-seek in the woods around the campsite, playing as they did when they were seven years old, maybe eight, in the school playground. They have let go of 'cool', let go of some of their defences. They are excited in a different way from the excitement of robbing the charity box. You might say that they are animated, living for the here and now.

Breathing

'Anima' is the spirit, the soul, the breath, the life. The practice of animation could inspire all informal education conversations. Informal educators in France and Italy are known as *animateurs*. In the United Kingdom, animateurs work mainly within arts-based community projects, and the link with youth workers is still developing.

Conversation is a step or two on from breathing, but really only just. Still, a conversation which ceases to be animated, which forgets that we have to breathe, is dead. Animation engages with movement and stirring, touching and probing, experimentation, repetition and unpredictability, rhythms which underlie speech. Playing–understood as the most significant vehicle of learning and development in childhood–can continue to inform aspects of learning in adolescence and in adult life. Imagination, which is such an important aspect of adolescence, can be understood as playing without props. Informal educators can access this aspect of adolescent development and make it a central aspect of developing conversations. In this, the practice of creativity is central. This can be seen particularly through the work of the imagination in arts-based learning.

Playing

Creativity has been marginalised in the routine practices of schooling, especially at secondary school level where the demands of national assessment prevail. Yet creativity is increasingly desired. It involves the capacity to imagine, to invent and to make new experiences as well as new artefacts/art works. It involves the much prized and rather easily trivialised ability to 'think outside the box'.

Creativity arises from the intellect and from the conscious mind, from discipline and striving. It demands practice. It also arises from gift, something discovered, something stumbled over. It requires the active, skilled and striving parts of the self, yet it also requires passivity and waiting. Discovering the right relationship between effort and non-effort needs to be practised over and over. There is the discipline of a particular piece of work, its conscious structure and framework, the shaping of a process of informal education. And there is hunch, intuition, going where the work takes you. Creativity needs both aspects of the self.

Activity is an essential aspect of any learning rooted in play. What might seem mere by-products of physiological growth, such as a baby's smile or roll in the cot, are learned through activity and repetition. Activity, repetition and imitation are the basis of social learning. The emphasis on activity in learning often goes hand in hand with models of education which focus on assessing skills development rather than knowledge, on the one hand, or values and moral development on the other. Playing involves energetic and exuberant movement: pushing and thrusting with my legs, jumping for joy, making an echo with my voice, banging a drum, throwing and returning. Movements are explored in play from infancy onwards. And repetition, repetition, repetition is the place where learning happens and knowledge of what the body can and cannot do is refined. A jump with this much effort will take me to the sandpit ... water poured will wet the sand and make it sticky. A great deal of play is bodily learning.

Another dimension of play involves pretending. Playing as pretending begins when children are two or three years old. Pretend play enables children to escape from the specific learning of their own bodies and capacities and to move, through play, into a sense of the wider world. Pretend play facilitates movement from the world of direct bodily experience into a world of symbols. When a child pretends for example to pour tea from an empty teapot he is creating access for himself to the concept of pouring. The child loosens the concept of pouring from his own activity to a wider frame of reference by pretending to pour. Through this wider frame of reference the child begins to participate in the wider culture. This aspect of playing as pretending is closely linked to the development of language.

Together, play and language are the vehicles of cultural mediation. Learning language enables the possibility of learning of rules of social existence, the rules of gender and all the other social interactions which constitute everyday life, not just for each individual child but for every child as a member of a family and a wider community.

Finally, play enables learning about emotions. Play is a specific use of 'transitional space' which enables us to connect the inner and the external world. This involves emotion as well as understanding, affect as well as cognition, to use the psychologists' terms. Play, like art forms and religious practice, assists integration by being a space which links each individual's relation to inner reality with that same individual's relation to external reality. Transitional spaces of various kinds enable increasing degrees of separation from the primary carer, usually the mother, in the early years. If rage and anxiety can be safely contained, it is also possible, through play, to discover the many ways that the excitement and liveliness of the body can become associated with the liveliness of ideas, words and other symbols and imagination.

In the early years of life, the space between the child and the body of the (m)other is the space in which play happens. Play becomes possible to the extent to which the baby has the opportunity to experience separation without abandonment. The state of being merged with the mother is replaced by the mother's adaptation to the baby's needs. This capacity for adaptation is also the basis on which trusting relationships come to be formed throughout life.

Discussion Point

All children (even some adults) remain to a lesser or greater degree capable of regaining the belief in being understood, and in their play we can always find the gateway to the unconscious and to the native honesty which so curiously starts in full bloom in the infant and then unripens to a bud. (Winnicott, 1964)

How much play is there in your work?

Through play the possibility of mutuality, of adaptation and of recognition of the child's needs is continuously explored, even in circumstances in which mothers and others fail (as they must) to perfectly respond and adapt to a child's needs. The affirmation of the possibility of trusting relationships is kept open. It is this which forms the basis of the child's approach to forming new relationships in adolescence. Play is exciting and also soothing. It is creative in its essence because it happens at the border between what can be objectively known (the outside world) and what is immediately accessible to the five senses, between the 'outside' and the 'inside'.

Arts-based animation/conversations

The development of arts-based informal education practice enables conversation, which, at its best, stays connected to these sources of creativity as they remain present during adolescence and into adult life. Arts-based practice demands concentration and effort. At the same time it can be sufficiently depersonalised to feel safe. Involvement in production and performance can highlight the extent to which the scripts of everyday conversation are exactly that: scripts which young people may have been given by teachers, or parents or other significant adults. Through involvement with the arts, they may recognise choices about whether or not they perform to the scripts that have been assigned to them. They can play safely with alternatives, either mainly with words, as in theatre, drama, fiction, poetry and stand-up, or with words playing a minor role in non-verbal forms of expression in dance, music and the visual arts. The examples that follow deliberately draw on some of the lesser known art forms, since the place of popular media–particularly DJ workshops, talent shows and video–as a starting point for youth work is well established.

Theatre and drama-based practice: what should she do now?

The work of Augusto Boal has inspired much animation-based practice. Called 'Theatre of the Oppressed', the method associated with Forum Theatre is closely affiliated with the liberatory pedagogy of Paolo Freire. As a method of popular theatre and popular education Boal's work suggests that 'actor' and 'theatre-goer' are not professional identities but can describe the identities adopted and developed by all of us every time we get dressed. Just like the children we once were in our 'pretend play', each time we get dressed, if you like, we dress up. We take on a role and a script offered to us by the culture we inhabit. Our identities and our performances are complicit in one another. While this usually happens relatively unconsciously, the methods of Forum Theatre enable the parts we play and the possible directions of the script to become available to consciousness. This sometimes makes clear what can change in the script and what is profoundly resistant to that change. The methods of Forum Theatre and its sister method, Invisible Theatre, involve actors investigating an ordinary situation and developing the action of the theatre out of the actions of everyday life.

Case Study

The actors came into a drop-in centre. They tried to find someone to talk to who could give them help with a letter someone had just received from Social Security. They caused a scene. They were not getting the help they needed. They drew attention to themselves and when they had everyone's attention, the next part of the scene continued. They revealed themselves to be actors and they called on the participation of the drop-in centre staff and the volunteers and the clients/users/members of the drop-in centre to ask: 'What should she do now?'

Clearly, the main character who had come in looking for help was not getting the help she was looking for, had become aggravated and was in danger of being asked to leave this open access provision. What, the actors ask, could these actors do differently? They could say hello, make her feel welcome, offer her a drink, someone says. OK, the actors say, we'll…

Show us how this scene might develop differently. For example, one of the young people who is using the drop-in centre, with much encouragement, comes forward to take part in the play. He acts out the role of a worker, saying hello to the person who has come with a letter, offering her a drink and a private place to talk. This scene is played again. OK, the actors ask, does the young person have the help she needs now? What should she do next? Play the scene again and this time, please, you come and take part.

A scene, or context, or question– 'How can these people get the support they need?'– can be played out again and again to enable the participants in services to improve practice, from the perspective of those who are marginal to it. More radically, the 'pretend play' of theatre can be used to imagine a world in which relations of dominance and subordination have disappeared.

The methods of Forum Theatre and Invisible Theatre are used primarily in situations where a group is facing external oppression. Cardboard Citizens, the homeless persons' theatre company, bases all its work on Forum Theatre methods. It is also possible to use the techniques of Forum Theatre to explore internalised oppression, in therapeutic work in closed groups. Theatre works as a method of transitional space linking external reality and the internal world of the emotions.

The act of transforming is transformatory. The spect–actor comes on stage and transforms the images that she sees and does not like–she transforms them into images she likes and desires, images of a just convivial society and in the act of taking the stage transforms herself into sculptor, musician, poet–in sum, entering the stage and showing her will in action, being the actor, being the protagonist, transforms herself into a citizen! (Cardboard Citizens Theatre Group)

In Forum Theatre the connections between the personal and social learning associated with 'pretend play' and the political, democratic learning of becoming a citizen are made explicit. However, many of the improvisation methods associated with Forum Theatre can be found among the exponents of the 'drama in education' movement. Some of the simplest improvisations can be used to develop and open up a continuing conversation in the context of youth and community projects, without any specific drama-related skills being required.

Conversations also emerge from more formal and scripted theatre, and the work of theatre-in-education companies such as Red Ladder can readily form part of a programme. There are also important alliances developing between mainstream arts organisations and community-based practice. The English National Opera, Opera North and the Welsh National Opera all run community-based programmes.

Case Study

The Royal Exchange Theatre in Manchester gave a group of lesbian and gay young people an experience whose memory will last a lifetime when they staged a production of *Romeo & Julian, Rosemary & Juliet*. Over a twelve-month period, 25 young people attended 12 Royal Exchange productions in both the main house and the studio. Between April and June 2005, the group devised *Romeo & Julian, Rosemary & Juliet*, which they subsequently performed to an audience of over 100 people in the Studio at the Royal Exchange. The project co-ordinator reported that young people, often for the first time, were able to explore their own experiences and–importantly–share them with each other. Telling one's story is perhaps one of the most powerful and life-changing events for many groups, but for LGBTQ (Lesbian, Gay, Bisexual, Trans, Questioning) young people who have long faced silence, invisibility, and at best tolerance, the power of telling their story is immense. Young people reported feelings of being in more control, feeling that there was somewhere to go, a renewed sense of purpose and–the key shift–that they did matter.

Dance

Both as a performing art and as a leisure activity dance participates in a variety of ways of connecting and exploring external and internal, subjective and objective realities. Many projects will offer dance as an alternative to football for girls, and street dance is increasingly offered as an option for boys. Youth workers working with parents, perhaps from strongly religious communities who view dancing as an inappropriate activity for their daughters, have been known to offer similar activities under the name 'Healthy movement'! Dance and movement offer possibilities for expression and communication, attraction and repulsion, in terms that go beyond words and intellect. Dance has been found especially valuable in the building of connection and communication between disabled and non-disabled participants and in particular with young people with learning disabilities.

The work of Klaus Compagnie in France involves integrating disabled and non-disabled dancers aged 12 and over. The company aims at 'democratising contemporary dance, giving both able-bodied and disabled people the opportunity to take part in an artistic activity, based on mutual respect, tolerance and open-mindedness'. They run workshops in open social and youth centres as well as in specialised workshops for disabled people, and are concerned with the mixing not only of performers but also of audiences. Dance professionals insist characteristically on a high standard of professionalism and precision, producing a high standard of improvisation and performance. In the very often segregated and 'specialist' area of work with young people with learning disabilities, dance sidesteps issues of intellectual ability and enables a high level of communication and participation. The Klepidistra project in Athens worked to devise a dance for the opening ceremony of the Special Olympics in Athens, which was broadcast all over the world.

As well as developing the standard of artistic skills such projects enhance the spirit of informal education, conversations promoting citizenship, mutual respect, tolerance and the open-mindedness which can bring people out of their 'silos' and into conversation. The work requires real self-denial too, as part of the exchange, insisting on the right to be different while retaining human dignity.

Music

Drums are often the most accessible instruments available to community groups. They offer an accessible and easy to learn beat and rhythm. Their associations are with stirring military emotions; marching bands rousing men to battle; or with secret communication across distances as with the secret 'tom-tom' which signalled the making and renewing of slave rebellions.

Case Study

As part of the peace process in Northern Ireland, workshops called 'A Different Drum' explored the use of the drum in Protestant and Catholic communities with members from both sides of the divide. In 1992, the founding members of Different Drums of Ireland, Stephen Matier and Roy Arbuckle, created a community arts project based on the simple concept of 'people marching to the beat of different drums'. Along with the builder and designer of the 'friendship drum', Paul Marshall, they created the Pelodaiko from a white oak Bushmills whiskey barrel. The name comes from the Romany word *pelo* meaning 'friend' or 'brother' and is based on the Japanese *taiko* family of drums. The unique aspect of workshops and performances by Different Drums of Ireland is their ability to bring together the Nationalist and Unionist symbolic drums–the Lambeg and the bodhrán–in a non-intimidating way for young people from either community.

The Ulfah Collective, part of Ulfah Arts in Birmingham, also uses drumming as the basis for bringing Muslim and non-Muslim women together for performances and workshops of 'pure harmony'. *Ulfah* means 'pure harmony', although the drummers accept cultural traditions which mean that women only use hand drums. This story is reminiscent of the founding of Abasindi drummers and dancers as part of the Abasindi women's co-operative in Manchester. In the context of much political and community-based work, Abasindi (the Swahili name means 'We are born to survive') also supported a cultural project which involved dancing, singing, costume-making and the playing of African percussion instruments. Initially respectful of tradition, the drumming was led at first by Nigerian master drummer Mr Tommy. However, in order to retain control of the women's co-operative, the women soon broke with tradition and decided that they would have to take up drumming themselves.

Voice workshops and singing are other vital forms of communication which require no additional equipment. Most cultures continue to value singing; British culture is an oddity in this respect. Unison singing, rounds, singing at the back of the bus–these are some resources to be drawn on. Embarrassment has to be overcome but nevertheless many people will enjoy the experience of singing when it is offered, and the community choirs movement continues to grow. After all, singing and breathing are closely linked in all people. Singing can carry celebration and sadness, praising and grieving, seriousness and silliness, if only narrowing and limiting cultural stereotypes can be abandoned.

Visual arts

The making of video and of digital photographs now accompanies everyday life and not only its high points of weddings and births. Young people and adults who do not have access to such technologies are excluded to a great extent from a significant aspect of contemporary citizenship. The making of DVDs accompanies the making of conversation in informal education just as snapshots record significant family events. Working with photography, film and digital images can enable exploration of the dominant visual themes of the culture. Projects on the visual have explored gendered representations; images of the body beautiful; and representations of young people themselves, especially through the scrutiny of hidden CCTV. Looking and being looked at now accompany much of life, and the ability of cultural work to animate and bring new life to this looking is a significant resource.

Such practice does not always develop smoothly, however. When filmmakers Hi8us North were working with a group of youngsters talking about their dreams on an estate in East Leeds, all of them were subject to Anti-Social Behaviour Orders. One lad, it was reported, said 'Your dreams are always something that will never happen–something you know you will never do.' Young people working with Hi8us were breaching the terms of their ASBOs which required them not to associate with each other. It was reported that the local Anti-Social Behaviour unit threatened to have them all arrested and sent to prison if they associated with one another in a film.

Another use of visual representations can be in exploring the art and artefacts that link particular communities and heritages or which affirm the artistic traditions of communities. A youth and community work project based in Blackburn was designed to explore the use of Paisley patterns and the link between these patterns and art from the Indian subcontinent. Another project explored and developed the use of calligraphy and traditions of non-representational art, linked to the work and signatures of graffiti artists.

As with all conversations, what the partnership between artists and informal educators requires is attention to words and to silence. In the context of arts-based work, it is particularly important to pay attention to narratives, symbols and metaphors, as places of 'pretend' in which young people can both move outside themselves and yet stay connected with themes that are of the utmost significance for them. Informal educators may sometimes be employed as playworkers concerned directly with providing opportunities for play to children. Even where this is not the case, they need to be concerned with themes of playfulness and imagination, through the conversations they provoke.

What is creativity?

Winnicott's account of the transitional space occupied by play is echoed in the account of 'the creative surrender' in the work of Marian Milner. In a series of remarkable books about her journal-keeping, Milner wrote about her findings that 'a certain kind of interior self-abnegation, deliberately practised, almost always opens up entirely new and unexpected possibilities of activity' (Milner, 1986). Milner describes an inner discipline and deliberate practice which is an adult and internalised version of the transitional space that Winnicott described in children's play.

From 1938, when she published *The Human Problem in Schools*, Milner spent her whole life attempting to promote new ways of education that were attentive to the whole self, to both the conscious and the unconscious mind. In 1982, at the end of her life, she would ask, as she went into schools once more:

How much would I find teachers helping their pupils to believe in and make use of this 'other mind' even if only in terms of the little people of the fairy tales who finish off one's work for one or even do the apparently impossible, in the night, provided one asks, and puts out a saucer of milk for them? And would this mean a lessening of the constant endeavour to din into people's heads enormous amounts of accumulated knowledge? Would it mean giving up trying to measure the success of this by means of examinations which a large proportion of them are bound to fail? In short, would I find anywhere that they were trying to teach the skills of non-effort in relation to effort, how to push conscious effort as far as it would go and then ask the 'other' mind to take over and, unlike Pilate, wait for an answer? (Milner, 1986)

Questioning the goals of the education system seems alien in a world obsessed with literacy and numeracy targets, with Standardised Attainment Tests and with Records of Achievement. Practices of measurement and reward are now also part of much learning outside school. There is no denying the importance of structure in informal learning, nor of effort, indeed of striving and of pushing effort as far as it will go. At the same time, this needs to be balanced with encouraging a practice of waiting and allowing space for individuals to find their own boundaries and limitations, and thereby perhaps to challenge and change them. One of the 'outcomes' which the best informal learning can offer is the pleasure involved in making so much effort that the sense of effort ceases and the young person 'loses themselves' in an activity. In the contemporary climate in education, it is all too easy for this practice of passivity and self-surrender to be forgotten

If such attention to the skills of non-effort is rare in formal schooling, it can sometimes be found in informal education settings and conversations. The real significance of the arts is that they are not merely leisure activities but activities that can return conversation to the spirit of play and animation.

Much formal and informal learning emphasises activity and striving, but for creativity to be present youth and community workers also need to learn to recognise and value 'passive surrender' as an aspect of learning.

Key Terms

The European tradition of informal educators as **animateurs** underlies the account of informal learning in this chapter. **Animation** can be creative-expressive engagement in the arts and also socio-cultural engagement of people in their communities through community associations and community development.

Further Reading

Boal, A. (2000) *Theatre of the Oppressed*. London: Pluto Press. This is the chief source for understanding Forum Theatre.

Lorenz, W. (1994) *Social Work in a Changing Europe*. London: Routledge. This gives a good account of the work of social pedagogues and animateurs in a European context.

Part III

Getting Deeper?
Reflection Points

- How much do you know about the histories and hopes of the families communities from which the young people you work with come? How culturally sensitive is your practice?
- What might be the benefits and what might be the negatives about setting up culturally specific groups or gender-specific groups in your youth work? What would be the rationale for undertaking identity-based work?
- Are the claims made about 'integrated provision' for work with young disabled people sound? How are young disabled people in your area benefiting from developmental informal education?
- Where are the safe spaces for young people? What makes them safe?
- Are you facilitating peer support in which young people can share experiences and solve problems that are identity-based?
- Do lesbian, gay, bisexual and transgender young people have access to adult role models in informal education settings?
- How can you tell that you are building up trusting relationships?
- What personal boundaries do you draw in your practice?
- In what way are you a friend to young people you work with and in what ways not?
- How do you enable young people to understand the meaning of the 'youth work' relationship?
- Are you an 'insider' or an 'outsider' in the communities of young people with whom you work?
- How are you using creativity and the arts in your practice?

Part IV

Unfinished Conversations

Silence, Bullying and Despair:
Youth Work Responses

- It is important to pay attention to silences, to what is not being said or what cannot be voiced.
- Finding a voice is an essential aspect of identity formation. Not being able to come to voice may be an indication of despair.
- Recognising and challenging bullying cultures and creating anti-bullying peer support and mediation is explored. Youth workers need the confidence to explore both anger and self-destructive feelings with young people.
- Informal educators have resources for responding to attempted suicide: being there, young-person-centredness, recognising the meanings of risky behaviour, openness to conversation about life and death.
- In responding to death and loss, youth workers will draw on their ability to recognise the breakdown of meaning and will support young people in a process of returning to voice and of reconstructing meaning.

'The quality of our silence is a real issue. There is a silence that is poisonous and evil – when someone is being silenced by someone else; a silence that is resentful because it is a bottling up of feelings that I can't trust myself to express and can't trust anyone else to listen to' (Williams, 2004: 107). And – as this chapter explores – there is the silence of despair, a condition in which speech about what matters to a person is impossible.

Attention needs to be paid to the silences as well as to the speech of young people, and, importantly, attention to the times when lack of speech points towards a condition of despair. The experience of being unable to find a voice is a common one in adolescence. When there is no available language in which to speak, or when there is fear or threat connected to the languages which *are* available, lack of voice may become closely connected with an experience of despair.

At times, young people lack a language or a context in which their personal conflicts and confusions can be explored. When speech and language seem to be failing, they may then begin to 'act out' or 'act in', somatise their pain, turning inner emotional or mental conflict back to or in on the body. Isolation and a sense of imprisonment accompany such silence. Youth workers working in multi-professional networks need to recognise when such oppressive silences exist and to create contexts and opportunities for this silence to be broken. Silences can be recognised both within group cultures and within individuals. There is a connection between immediate experiences of group pressure or bullying, and attempted suicide.

In speaking of 'bullying cultures', there is a recognition of the presence of 'the bullier' and 'the bullied' as potential roles for all who take part in group activities. It is part of the role of the youth and community worker to intervene to shift such patterns and dynamics.

Bullying and mediation

There are times when silence may seem preferable to the available words. What is a bullying culture? There is not always a rigid distinction between the 'bully' and 'bullied'. Both may be present in a single young person who seeks the protection of a group in order to avoid being bullied and then finds him/herself involved in maintaining an existing cultural prejudice against gays or slags or nerds or Asians or some other group. In order to recognise a bullying culture, it is necessary to analyse the operation of labels which categorise and exclude. Such labels may be attached to supposedly deviant sexuality, to intelligence, to disability and to racialised identities, to name just some of the most common patterns. A common motive for adopting bullying behaviour which isolates, traps or victimises outsiders, and those who do not belong to a group, is that it provides a protection against being bullied oneself. It provides a sense of safety. One young person reported to LEAP, the national training network for anti-bullying projects:

Discussion Point

I used to be seen as a nerd, I used to get attacked in clubs and parks. People used to take advantage. So I decided to get on with the people who were doing the bullying. I had to become a bully myself, but I felt safe.

How would your practice respond to this young person?

Work undertaken by youth workers can enable people to feel safe in ways that do not depend upon threatening and intimidating others. Resources for responding to threats of violence are now seen as fundamental to training and development. Peer support and peer mediation are among the most important of the strategies deployed. The development of skills in peer mediation often begins in the transition year between primary and secondary education. If skills are developed in confronting difficulties assertively early in life, these can be carried forward into the more complicated territory of adolescence.

Mediation is a method of communicating in which people who are in disagreement are enabled to talk to one another and find ways of working out their problems. Mediators do not give advice or offer solutions but enable the parties involved in disagreement to find their own answers to problems. The involvement of young people as mediators is important as it enables trust, safety and an acknowledgement of the significance of any dispute in a different way from the involvement of adults. When peer mediation works well, there are opportunities for each person involved to tell their story from their own point of view, and have it taken seriously. There is also a commitment to win-win outcomes, seeking compromises and settlements which enables everyone involved to gain what they need, rather than what they want, to move forward for the future. It is essential that mediation relationships are voluntary: that everyone involved chooses to take part and this does not happen under duress. The process of mediation is impartial and non-judgmental. It is important that mediators do not take sides and do not pronounce judgements. They need to develop a strong sense of their own independence. This may mean working outside their own friendship group in order to be sure that they are not connected to the parties in the dispute.

The development of such qualities and skills in young people needs the direction, input and support of a relationship with an adult informal educator whose role is to act as coach to the mediators and to assist them in identifying problems (Luxmoore, 2000).

Fight, flight and flow

A number of clear frameworks are used to assist young people in becoming peer mediators and in the development of responses to conflict. The most commonly used of these is 'Fight, flight and flow'. The most common, usually described as instinctive, responses to perceived threat or attack are 'fight' and 'flight'. Fighting escalates a conflict and seeks to resolve and end it through the defeat of the opponent. Flight seeks to end conflict by running away: through avoidance it offers a means of escape and survival. Both fight and flight are essentially means of self-protection. Each has significant uses for survival. Not all threats and conflicts are immediately life-threatening, however. Conflict mediation training attempts to offer an alternative to 'fight' and 'flight' by providing a moment to pause and seek a new direction, a 'flow' which may enable a conflict to be worked through and more creative ways forward to be found. It is all in the 'pause', the moment of stillness, between impulse and action.

Approaches from conflict mediation, such as assertiveness, can be used in work with individuals too. These include identifying and listening out for particular conversational styles, such as wind-ups, put-downs, blaming and 'enemy thinking'. In all this, the exploration of anger and its meanings for individuals and groups is vital.

Anger

Silence, a repressed and brooding silence or a silent coldness, can convey anger as powerfully as a slammed door and more powerfully than many words. Anger can be hot, but in silence is often cold, intended to break connection. An angry resentful silence may also exist because it seems impossible to find words.

Both the young person and the youth and community worker can become aware of what triggers an angry response as well the traps which can be sprung in banter and 'jokey' conversations. Together they can devise strategies either for avoiding them or for enabling conflict to be worked through or deflected more easily. This practice also involves recognising personal attacks: statements which judge, undermine, blame or attack a person rather than their behaviour. 'You smell ....' 'Your clothes are scruffy ....' 'Your hair's a mess ....' Or more subtly: 'You're always late.' 'You never do the washing up.' 'You're just like your mother.'

It is possible to learn to recognise the patterns of interaction which are particularly hurtful. Such patterns occur not only between individuals but also between groups. Alongside personal individualised attacks, people are regularly bullied or harassed because of their membership of a group. 'They're so mean ... they're dirty ... they don't look after their children ... they are taking our jobs/our houses/our women.' Young people need support in responding to such projections, which are often visceral and involve a feeling of physical repulsion. Feeling angry at and hurt by such prejudice and rejection is inevitable: the youth worker needs to work to offer the 'pause' in which these feelings can be acknowledged in order to enable the movement beyond 'fight' or 'flight'.

Exploring the roots of anger means taking time to recognise a young person's silence or their angry outbursts. It means making time to spend with individuals outside the group contexts of conversation. Youth workers need to recognise that there are matters which young people may not yet be able to bring to voice but which are nevertheless of great significance. The skilled youth and community worker works at a boundary with counselling and therapy, offering informal support as well as informal education.

The main difference between the disciplines of youth and community work and counselling on the one hand and psychotherapy on the other is the therapist's training and capacity to work with unconscious material. Youth and community workers need to expect at times to work with young people who are experiencing high levels of conflict, distress and anger and they need to be well prepared for this. Physical release of tension may be an issue. It can be useful to offer alternative physical expressions of anger that can prevent the tension building up in a young person, an alternative use for the 'boxercise' equipment in the gym which a youth project uses. This can offer a diversion from self-destructive or other destructive actions. But diversion is not enough. The youth work relationship needs to be about development.

One method of understanding 'anger' – of both the 'seeing red' and the 'ice cold' variety – is to see anger as a means of disguising other feelings and to attempt to discover the other feelings which the anger disguises. Anger is often a response to perceived injustice; it is also a response to threat and insult. It can cover over sadness; it can also cover over fear. It is important to try to discover what it is that is causing a young person to be afraid, and what needs they are seeking to meet.

Self-destructive feelings

Another pattern of responding to oppression follows a self-destructive course. Challenging self-destructive beliefs (especially what are termed 'should, must, ought to and have to beliefs') and put-downs of the self as well as put-downs of others is significant. 'I should lose weight.' 'I must deserve the treatment I am getting.' 'I ought to be fitter than I am.' 'I have to ...' Such self-destructive beliefs often link to a punitive voice inside a young person (termed by some psychologists a 'punitive superego') and may sometimes connect to self-harm, eating disorders or other forms of extreme emotional distress. There is a difference between acting in response to an external authority which has been internalised and acting from an authentic inner authority. Youth work needs to support young people in developing an authentic inner authority. It is possible to highlight and explore such 'should' statements in conversation and then investigate the extent to which a young person feels able to make choices about their situation and to express themselves assertively.

Attempted suicide

These struggles in inner and outer speech continue to be present even when young people are at the extreme point of attempting suicide. Suicide accounts for 30 per cent of deaths in the 15 – 24 age group. One of the main indicators of serious suicidal intent is the existence of more than one attempt. This means interventions after a first unsuccessful attempt at suicide have a real life-saving quality.

Discussions of young people's mental and emotional health often refer to aspirations which have long been characteristic of youth and community work. A Mental Health Foundation Report (1999) *Bright Futures*, suggested that a young person is emotionally healthy when they are able to develop psychologically, creatively, intellectually, spiritually and emotionally. Signs of this include: the ability to sustain and develop mutual relationships; enjoying solitude; empathising with others; playing and learning; developing a sense of right and wrong; and resolving and learning from problems.

Each story of attempted suicide has its own unique trajectory. Each story suggests the absolute uniqueness of each adolescent crisis. Equally, the crisis can often be recognised as a crisis with life and death significance. The meaning-making available to us, the languages we have to speak about life and death matter. During the period which precedes a suicide attempt, the way forward from childhood into a well-established adult life may seem blocked. Death seems to be the only way of bringing a crisis to a conclusion. This can be acute for lesbian and gay young people in contexts in which the only paths to successful adulthood that appear to be on offer are heterosexual (Ben-Ari and Gil, 1998). Telling stories about crises and ways of surviving them is important. Working to help people construct their own narratives as a way of making meaning and making sense is central to informal education. The presence of adults who can tell stories which show how adolescent crises can be successfully negotiated and who can act as mentors is also important.

Factors which have been commonly found among triggers of attempted suicide include isolation, bullying and the experience of coercion or abuse in intimate family relationships. This can include bullying by siblings, domestic violence, strict emotional and financial control as well as rape and other forms of sexual exploitation and abuse. Experiences of abandonment and neglect may be invoked in by the ending of romantic and/or sexual relationships.

Responses to attempted suicide which offer support in the process of recovery are also responses which characterise youth and community work at its best. These include practices of 'being there'; situatedness/starting where young people are; coming to voice and conversation; learning to recognise risky behaviour; openness to exploring the meanings associated with life and death.

Being there

It is impossible to know how many suicides have been prevented by this simple and basic human activity. 'Being there' refers not so much to mere physical togetherness and proximity, although that is certainly the thinking behind the 24-hour suicide watch in prisons. It is much more a matter of quality of presence. It need not even be the 'unconditional positive regard' of person-centred counselling. It is more simple. It involves the basic recognition of the life of the suicidal person and the holding of that life in a relationship. That such 'holding' can be performed by strangers was brilliantly recognised by the late Chad Varah, the founder of the Samaritans. It requires no special qualifications or training as it is a fundamental human activity. It requires time, consistency and attentiveness. The regular existence of a group in which important matters are discussed and in which you know it matters to others that you are there is a crucial example of 'being there'. Knowing that, if you turn up at a certain place or time, the person you are hoping or expecting to see will be there, is reassuring and supportive. In the context of attempted suicide, these aspects of practice take on a life or death quality. They act in the here and now as a reassurance that life goes on, in a context and at a time for the suicidal young person when such simple matters are far from certain. 'Being there' is a *sine qua non* of any recovery process. Its importance is inestimable (Collander Brown, 2005).

In the presence of another person who demonstrates this attentiveness, it may be possible for trust to develop over a period of time. This developing trust can enable a survivor of attempted suicide both to name their experience and to experience an attentive response rather than a censuring, punitive one. Attempted suicide is an experience which is extremely difficult to voice as it remains the source of a great deal of shame in many families and communities. It is therefore possible for it to remain a 'dark secret' for many years. It is covered over with colloquialisms and euphemisms. 'I hope you're not going to do anything silly.' 'Don't worry, I'm not going to do anything silly.' This euphemism shows how hard it is, how taboo, even to speak about the attempt on one's own life. Suicide remains taboo even when it is no longer a crime. This is because it is a breach of the fundamental connectedness of life in community. Perhaps, as the individualism of society intensifies, it will become less of a taboo. The existence of a taboo represents the persistence of a belief in the sacredness of life. Yet, paradoxically, the existence of taboo, by preventing the experience of attempted suicide from being voiced, can make recovery more difficult. The existence of taboo often prevents something coming to voice, and not just in relation to suicidal feelings; informal educators need to be keenly aware of the powerful existence of taboo areas which effectively silence young people and control their development.

It may not be possible initially for a person recovering from a suicide attempt to do more than name what has happened. But even one opportunity to have their recent experience, their brush with death, named and recognised makes an inestimable difference as it challenges the silence and secrecy in which such attempts are shrouded. Just as the secrecy and shame may produce the conditions in which a further suicide attempt seems the only way forward, so recognition and coming to voice are important factors in creating the conditions for recovery.

Recognising risky behaviour/edginess

Attempted suicide is commonly part of a continuum of risky/life-threatening behaviour. It seems that this is unconsciously driven and not evident to the individual but that nevertheless people around him or her have a sense that his or her behaviour is out of control. Some of this behaviour may be conventionally risky and visible; other behaviour may be internalised and profoundly invisible to others. Swallowing bleach, threatening to jump off bridges, storing tablets for overdoses, walking down the middle of the road, seeking unsafe sex with strangers, binge drinking, and taking recreational drugs in excessive quantities are examples. But so are more private rituals of despair, surrounding eating or cleaning or religion or fitness, which may be less visible or even appear praiseworthy to those around them. Suicidal intent may not be conscious, but a pattern is clear which indicates that issues of life and death may as well be left to chance, that life is hopeless and meaningless. There is a 'cry for help'.

It may be that the young person who is suicidal does not recognise the dangerousness of the situation they are in, and that they provoke feelings of anger and contempt from helpers rather than empathy and kindness. Even where it is hard to attend to feelings because they are largely unconscious in the person concerned, it may be possible to attend to behaviours and help them minimise risk. 'I will not buy paracetamol.' 'I will not drink after midnight.' These cognitive strategies for harm reduction also enable an individual to regain a sense of control over their actions and so regain a sense of hope. This in itself can begin a process of restoring a sense of purpose in living.

Hopelessness is a key factor in the conditions for attempted suicide. People who have a relationship with someone who is suicidal have a significant role in providing a feeling of hope until such time as that person can provide hope for themselves. Helping a person take small steps which limit self-destructive behaviour is a good example of providing a framework in which hope can be rekindled. One of the real difficulties of the adolescent transition is that it may well be the very first time that a young person has faced a crisis of life/death significance, or at least the first time they have been aware of it. They therefore have no earlier experience to draw on, and part of the support that can be offered by adult others is that they can represent and somehow 'stand in for' the belief that transition, even through a life/death crisis, is indeed possible.

Youth and community work and 'being there'

Informal education is about being as well as doing. Many peer groups in which young people can find themselves do not feel safe. But a chosen group facilitated by an adult worker, particularly if it can include young men/women who have been pushed to the edge in various ways in other settings, is of enormous value. Such a group may be rooted in exploration of particular faith or cultural identities. It may be a single-sex group.

It might be a peer support group for lesbian, gay, bisexual and questioning young people. Or it might be a mixed group, a group based on a shared cultural interest such as music or drama or film or photography, or an inter-faith, inter-cultural group. The quality of the group of significance here is that it is a regular, reliable group, is not short term, here today and gone tomorrow, and that it starts where young people are with their interests and experiences. It is a comfortable and warm space and a place in which an individual feels cared for, recognised for who they are and therefore able to explore things that are important to them.

If a peer group conversation can be established, it may become possible for aspects of a young person's risk-taking behaviour to be open to scrutiny and discussion, by themselves and others as well as by the youth and community worker. Youth and community work can involve the introduction by the worker to young people of the idea of responsible risk-taking. In this context it may be possible to offer opportunities for taking risks and an experience of dangerousness in a more controlled environment. Outdoor education has traditionally been a very important element of youth and community work practice and offers a number of possibilities. Taking risks may – at one extreme – be about confronting and testing out the desire to die without actually dying. It may also be a way in which the reliability of others can be tested and the capacity of others to 'be there for us' can be checked.

The practice of hopefulness

The silence of anger and despair or the existence of self-destructive beliefs and behaviour patterns and language is something to which all who work with young people in informal settings need to be alert. The ordinary experience of adolescence can be difficult in its own right. It can involve feelings of depression and loss, associated with separation, or feelings of the inability to separate, of merging, being overwhelmed and taken over. In each case, the existence of a feeling of life/death significance may emerge, simply because some aspect of earlier relationships metaphorically 'has to die' in order for new patterns to emerge and adult identity to develop (Winnicott, 1971). It is important to recognise too that during the period of adolescence, the question 'Do I want to live?' and 'What is the point of life?' are existential questions of great urgency for many people who are not necessarily suicidal.

Death, loss and grief

When death and loss happen, as they do throughout life, boundaries shift and change. At the moment of crisis, boundaries break down, all meaning seems to disappear and new meanings have to be created. The tasks of grieving are understood in a variety of ways but are always thought to include:

- the need to accept the reality of loss;
- the need to recognise, acknowledge and work through the pain caused by that loss;
- the need to adjust to an environment in which the reality of the loss is permanent;
- the need to move on in life, to invest energy in new relationships.

The impact of the death of young people on their peer groups, and on the youth workers and indeed other professionals who work with them, is something which deserves much more attention.

One youth worker, Pam Wilson, spoke of how her relationships with young people were changed for ever by the death of a young man following a car accident. During the hours after the news of his death reached the Youth Centre, all the existing patterns of provision changed. The staff recognised they wanted and needed to 'be there' for the young people.

> **Case Study**
>
> 'We just went straight to the Youth Centre and opened the doors. The young people started to come in ... we were all in shock. He was such a lovely young man. Even though it was a Saturday, Easter Saturday, we just opened the doors and everyone came and we just sat and talked and talked. The young people used the Club facilities to make the laminated signs for the shrine on the road where he died. There was enormous quietness, enormous stillness. We hosted the gathering after the funeral at the Youth Centre. There are some young people in that group who I will never, never lose touch with.'

Workers who have the confidence to work with young people's life narratives and meaning-making will also, we might hope, have the confidence to be there with them at times of death and loss, when the meaning breaks down, and to offer a framework within which the beginnings of a process of meaning-reconstruction can occur (Thompson, 2002).

Key Terms

Despair might be understood as a sense of the ultimate meaninglessness, worthlessness, and purposelessness and pain of life, culminating in death. It is the opposite of **hope**, and informal learning is a courageous practice capable of building up hope.

Loss includes the experience of death and bereavement, but also refers to loss of close relationships as a result of divorce or separation of parents, loss of early romantic partners and close friends, and loss of self as a result of abuse, illness or disfigurement.

Further Reading

Cowie, H. and Wallace, P. (2000) *Peer Support in Action: From Bystanding to Standing By.* London: Sage.

Fine, N. and Macbeth, F. (1992) *Playing with Fire: Training in the Creative Use of Conflict*. Leicester: National Youth Agency.

Piper, D.E. (2007) *Young People, Suicide and Self-Harm*. Brighton: TSA.

Spandler, H. and Warner, S. (2007) *Beyond Fear and Control: Working with Young People Who Self-harm*. Manchester: 42nd Street.

These texts all offer resources for developing practice which responds to young people's experience of bullying, of abuse, of conflict and of despair.

Silence, Spirit and Solidarity: Resources for Practice

- Isolation and exclusion is a form of punishment. It can however also be a means of escape. Youth workers need to have confidence in supporting young people in making the break from oppressive peer groups.
- The other side of loneliness is solitude. Solitude is a powerful resource for youth workers to offer all young people, including those recovering from extreme abusive experiences.
- Access to experiences of awe and wonder through youth work opportunities in outdoor education, retreats and residentials can enable a recognition of the power of solitude.
- Solitude and solidarity are linked: there is an opening up to a greater sense of connectedness and compassion through such experiences.
- Models of faith development can be useful to youth workers exploring these experiences with young people.
- The fears associated with loneliness as well as the capacity to retain a sense of being loved even when alone need to be understood in this aspect of informal education.

Loneliness and solitude

Belonging and attachment are bare necessities of life. The need to belong to our own particular group is being intensified in the context of globalisation and what has been called 'MacWorld'.

The experience of not belonging can be quite devastating. Feelings of rejection, of being a misfit, arise and this painful experience may then be taken as a mark of identity. Something about 'you' just does not fit and this 'something' can be felt to be unchangeable. Just at the point at which 'you' (the subject of this exclusion) have succeeded in fitting in, the rules change. You are a 'marked man'. And the marking becomes a problematic or difficult feature of identity. Skin colour can be used to mark an outsider, as can voice and speech, parts of the body and dress. The name 'weirdo' passed around a group can be attached to any feature, normal or abnormal, common or unusual.

Informal educators working with peer groups sometimes develop a sense that it is good for some young people who have been excluded as peers to be included. Conversely, it is better for some young people to leave destructive peer groups. Some young men and women need support in letting go of groups and experiences that have been oppressive to them and in which they have been marginalised.

Isolation is commonly used as a form of punishment and a form of torture. In such instances, isolation is a deliberate denial of what is needed in a nurtured and nurturing self. But in other instances, temporary isolation may be exactly what is needed in order for someone both to escape from and come to terms with hurtful and damaging aspects of experience, before re-engaging with others.

In the context of supportive youth work programmes, the other side of isolation and deliberate exclusion can be explored. For it has another side, which opens out into a sense of oneness and unity. To be able to be alone, to enjoy solitude and to enjoy one's own company is a capacity that is currently very under-developed and under-valued. To be content to be alone and in one's own company is to be able to acknowledge and recognise the fears of desertion, abandonment and loneliness that are part of the human condition. People with a highly developed capacity for solitude are often people who have turned traumatic experiences of isolation into a well. For a young person who has experienced acute trauma or loss or has been oppressed through bullying or other forms of abuse, informal education processes which offer peak experiences can give access to a counter-experience of joy in the context of what will often have been extreme experiences of pain and suffering. Some of these peak experiences, to use a term from the 'growth movement' and from transpersonal psychology, are achieved through celebration and collaboration with others. Others are more solitary and it is the opportunities offered by solitude that are explored here.

Wildness in nature

Peak experiences may be associated very strongly with the experience of 'nature', especially with wildness in nature. There is an intense form of seeing and recognising the presence of the natural world which enables us to put our own lives in a different perspective. Most seeing is an experience of verbalising and commenting, in order to notice and remember. But there is another kind of seeing which involves a letting-go. 'When I see this way,' the poet and nature writer Annie Dillard writes, 'I am transfixed and emptied' (Dillard, 1975: 40).

Such extreme experiences can be seen as experiences of ego-less-ness and in that place experiencing the sense of the givenness/the gift of love.

The sense of awe and wonder is a universal human stance which does not rely on religious faith. There is a sense of the smallness of the ego in relation to the vastness of the 'other'. There is a sense of a relationship of dependency on the 'other', not as a threatening place but as a place in which it is possible to receive love. Although the description of such experiences can make them sound esoteric and rare, I think in fact that they are quite common and available to all. The tradition of outdoor education in youth work, so much associated in the past with building 'toughness' and in the present with 'management and leadership training', has the capacity to open out to such experiences.

Outdoor education and solitude

There is nothing more awe inspiring than sleeping out of doors in a wild place on a cloudless night and seeing the stars. There can be little that is more wonderful than watching the dawn from a place high on a mountain or from a cliff overlooking the sea. Outdoor education is commonly used to teach teamwork and other management skills. Yet it might be possible to reclaim these outdoor education traditions in the name of what the rock climber Jim Perrin has called 'radical joy'.

Perrin (2006) describes, in the chapter 'The Vision of Glory', climbing Beinn a Chaoruinn, the Hill of Rowan, a mountain above Loch Moy. The winter day begins dully, but near the summit, suddenly 'the mist is scoured with speed from the face of the mountain' and Perrin sees out over the surrounding peaks and corries 'all glitter and coruscation, shapes of the Mamores beyond a phantasmal ivory gleam'. Perrin's account develops into a meditation on the power of such visionary moments – 'the occasional goings through into the white world, the world of light' – to call out a goodness in us. 'Our essential life, the joy-life, is a sequence of these moments: how many of us could count even sixty such?'

For Perrin, taking the high ground does not lead one to superiority or righteousness but to humility. 'I was annihilated,' he writes of an experience on Jacob's Ladder in the Peak District. 'I had no existence but simply looked out at the inconceivable beauty of the world that had detached me from any concept of self in order that I might see.'

The naming of such experiences comes later. Travellers return from the heights and tell stories in ways that give clues that such experiences happen, that the 'highs' are accessible to all. Nature and the outdoors are a resource for practice, as are the travellers' tales of such experiences in poetry and in the mystical traditions of world faiths: the Kabbalah, the Sufi, Yoga, Shamanism, contemplative prayer.

Alongside a sense of awe and wonder comes a desire to care for the environment. The John Muir Trust has developed a series of 'awards' which can be undertaken by youth groups, which emphasise learning through the exploration of wilderness places. They encourage discovery, exploration, conservation and sharing.

Residentials and retreats

Youth workers have for a long time used residentials, camping trips, and fishing expeditions as a method for exploring such themes, including retreats which contain a good deal of the practice of silence. The practice of separation from the ordinary, everyday routines in order to enable a sharper awareness and a sharper pattern of understanding to break through is a time-honoured method.

In the context of traditions of youth and community work as activism, 'retreat' can sound disempowering. It suggests a withdrawal from the struggles of life and from the struggle with injustice. It might also suggest an over-preoccupation with the self or with religion as a comforting but ultimately false diversion from reality, an 'opium of the people', offering 'pie in the sky' as an alternative to struggle for justice, which is abandoned under the mumbo-jumbo of new age mysticism. A recognition of the part played by the practice of retreat houses of all faith traditions in building up solidarity, generosity and hospitality, challenging the boundaries of inclusion and often extending hospitality to people – including young people that mainstream public sector funded services fail to engage – can counter this negative view.

A secular form of this practice is found in the tradition of maintaining an 'outdoor centre' for use by young people's groups on 'residentials'. Such residential experiences have long been recognised as offering a great deal to young people who are in the process of establishing themselves as independent adults. They require planning and preparation. There is much opportunity for informal learning throughout the process of creating a residential experience. Residentials can offer the opportunity for exploring solitude and solidarity, a taste of the wilderness experience.

The Outward Bound movement was a significant early influence in the development of youth and community work. The movement's slogan was: 'We are better than we know' and its founder, Kurt Hahn based his movement on the belief in learning through new and challenging experiences. 'It is a sin of the soul to force young people into opinions – indoctrination is of the devil – but it is culpable neglect not to impel young people into experiences.' Some of these experiences involve self-confrontation and pain and loss. This is a story Hahn recounted from his early work on Outward Bound:

Discussion Point

A boy kept in on his own in the holidays after some wrongdoing made a sculpture. 'Why did you never do this at school? Why did you never do this before?' I asked him. He gave me the devastating answer 'I can only do these things when I am sad, and here I had no opportunity for being sad.' (Kurt Hahn (1965) on Outward Bound)

Are there times in your practice when young people feel free to feel unhappy?

In a culture which frequently seems to be in denial of the reality of pain and loss, such a recognition of the significance of feelings of sadness in what has often been taken to be a masculine context in which feelings are denied, is salutary.

Solitude and solidarity

Out of the depths of self in solitude it is possible to experience a sense of self in solidarity which goes far beyond self and can be termed transpersonal. The profound connection between self and other, between solitude and solidarity, has been noted by mystics in all the world faith traditions. Solidarity is a process in which the boundaries of the ego are opened. It is very different from empathy or fellow feeling in which the boundaries of the ego are in fact strengthened. Solidarity arises in a place of openness which is also a place of joy, but this openness is often in a place which has been created by wounding and hurt. Solitaries come to solidarity with the world especially in its brokenness, alienation and poverty. One does not so much 'do' solitude as 'be' it: in being solitary, it is said, one welcomes the interrelatedness of beings in the compassion of love. Solidarity is both a recognition of the otherness of the other and connectedness with the other. Luce Irigaray's formulation 'I love (to) you' represents this sense of solidarity in which there is a pause, a space, a gap.

Experiences of oneness, solidarity and wonder may be identified by people in many contexts and in a range of settings. One young man I know talks about his experience of deep sea diving as the place in which he felt most himself, surrounded by beauty and peace. He is an inner city schoolboy with no immediate access to the sea, but his experience and memories of this reality are as powerful to him as his everyday realities of school and family life. The more extended opportunities made available through retreats or residentials or outdoor education for stillness, solitude and wonder need to link to opportunities to be still and quiet in the everyday urban context too.

Many of the educational practices discussed earlier in this book are based on a recognition of hurt as part of young people's experience and it is good if these practices can also enable young people to engage with these experiences of solidarity. They can open up to wonder and delight. Quite often the naming of experience that has been silenced is painful and troubling. It can however also draw out new forms of recognition, and a crossing of borders into new experience. Such transformations may involve the need to take 'time apart' from existing relationships to experience connection in a new way.

The difference between loneliness and solitude is worth investigating. The development of an ability to be alone and to draw nourishment from this is an aspect of informal education and informal support. A new understanding can lead to a sense of loss of existing patterns and relationships even when there is also the glimpse of new possibilities, the wondering and delight at new connections and new relationships to be made. Youth work in a climate which over-emphasises activities and achievement can all too easily become neglectful of the emotional work which the emancipatory changes arising from education may entail.

In some societies the sense and the role of being 'set apart' in order to undertake some particular work has been immensely important. Such 'being set apart' can be associated with 'holy men and women' but the space of separation also represents a space for critical consciousness, for artists and for those who are called to 'prophetic action'. Being able to support young people who may be set apart in some way is a skilled task which requires both wisdom and discernment on the part of informal educators. There is – to put it simply – a very fine line between holiness and craziness – and it will no doubt seem safer to many not to dabble in these waters, at the edge of this sea.

It is not possible for young people to recognise these matters of basic orientation to the world and its meanings until they are given the opportunity to explore them. In faith-based youth work such experiences are most likely to be acknowledged; there is a language for depicting, for example, the changing understanding of God which accompanies human development.

Faith development

Some of this has been codified into an understanding of 'developmental stages': stages of 'faith development'. In particular, it has been codified to chart the change between an affiliative faith and a searching faith. Affiliative faith refers to a faith of later childhood/early adolescence when it is belonging that matters. In this stage, the affiliations of one's family and other important adults such as teachers and youth and community workers are immensely important. The stories told in the faith or ethical traditions are also important, as is allegiance to rules laid down for behaviour. This is clearly relevant to understanding the success of such organisations as Brownies, Cubs, Guides, Scouts and Woodcraft Folk, for whom the establishing of rules and structures are explicit. This also enables us to understand how the Scout movement has proved attractive as a basis for organisation to, for example, Muslim and Sikh groups seeking to develop youth provision.

The model also suggests why such organisations tend to go into steep decline during later adolescence. Affiliative faith, it is suggested, is replaced in later adolescence and early adulthood by a searching faith. Searching faith has doubt and questioning at its core. It needs to experiment; to test out alternatives and ways of understanding the world. The need for commitment is felt sharply in this faith stage and individuals search out persons or causes to commit themselves to.

In this sense, faith transitions are not significantly different from other aspects of transition associated with identity formation.

The meanings associated with belonging to a faith tradition will be very different for Christians and non-Christians in a Christian-dominated culture. The automatic designation 'C of E' for those who profess no religious allegiance is continuing evidence of this dominance. One of the effects is to make it more difficult for people of non 'C of E' faith communities (including Roman Catholics, and members of independent Protestant denominations) to accept that there is a time to abandon or leave behind affiliative faith. Affiliative faith requires an explicit commitment to a faith community and offers the protection of that community to all who belong to it. Letting go of or questioning belonging may be a very risky business for people who already have a sense of needing to surviving in a hostile culture. There is a sense of dangerousness. It may seem to involve letting go of both parental protection and the protection of the community.

There is a question therefore about the progressive and stage nature of developmental models. Perhaps it is possible to question and search while continuing to belong. It is one of the roles of faith-based youth work to enable this to happen. A significant method for enabling this is through the experience of silence and solitude.

Dangers of manipulation and 'brainwashing'

All involved in informal education need to be aware of the dangers presented by extreme religious and political groups who are capable of manipulating these 'edgy' states that are vivid in adolescence. One student chaplaincy offers the following sensible advice:

A destructive religious group is usually characterised by the following:

- A leader who claims divinity or an extraordinary relationship with God
- A leader who is the sole judge of a member's actions or faith
- Totalitarian governance
- Totalistic control over members' daily lives
- Exclusivity and isolation
- Development of unhealthy emotional dependence
- Prohibition of analysis and critical thinking
- Utilization of methods of ego destruction and mind control
- Exploitation of members' finances
- Exploitative working conditions which discourage the full use of one's abilities
- Discouragement of free and independent pursuit of education (Manchester student chaplaincy leaflet)

As the writers say, 'When you're hurting – or even when you're not – beware of people with answers to all life's questions.'

Fear of solitude

Solitude can be frightening because it is a place of self-knowledge before it can be a place of self-acceptance. Many people are frightened of being on their own and of being away from the distractions that being with other people can bring. They are fearful of having a painful reality about their lives made apparent when they are alone. So they seek to keep busy, to find company, in order to avoid facing up to difficulties which may be all too real when they are alone. For people with a capacity for solitude, however, there is a sense of restfulness and of taking a break from the demands and perceptions of others.

The capacity for solitude derives primarily from an experience of satisfying and loving connection with others. Solitude is different from loneliness because whereas loneliness is the experience of abandonment, solitude can be enjoyed because you have already experienced, in Winnicott's words, 'being alone when someone else is present'. This is literally the case for the baby who learns experientially to tolerate his/her mother's absence because her return can be relied upon. The child internalises a sense of the mother and the feelings of safety that go with that, while the mother is temporarily absent. So, at the heart of each of us there is a sense of relationship.

'There is no such thing as a baby', said Winnicott, enigmatically pointing to the presence always of the 'nursing couple', the caretaker–child relationship from the beginning of life. This sense of continuing connectedness, even in the absence of others, is not the same thing as memory. It is an internalised state, which derives from the 'taking in' of the love of (an) (m)other, rather as we take in food. And, like the nourishment that comes from food, the connection with others needs to be renewed. As the sense of connection is renewed, solitude can be deepened.

Loneliness on the other hand is a state of abandonment and the absence of love and is an acute form of suffering. Hence, solitary confinement is used as an extreme punishment; 'naughty children' are sent away from others to their rooms, outside the classroom, to the 'naughty step'. The feeling of abandonment, the feeling of lack and of being without, is one of the fiercest and most desperate of human states. In loneliness, we re-experience those states of abandonment that have been with us since infancy. Without the other, the self is endangered, perhaps permanently. So the other must be clung on to, never let go of, if they do return.

On the other hand, being alone, for some people, is a necessary survival mechanism. 'Alone' is where you learn to be safe from the dangers posed by others, where you are able to exercise a certain amount of self-protection, to hold on to the self within certain boundaries. It is a place of recuperation. At times this same mechanism of separating in order to survive can act as a mask, creating a split between an outer self and an inner anguish. For young people the experience of fear of breakdown during adolescence can lead to a development of this 'masking' strategy, which makes depression so hard to recognise.

In Winnicott's account of the capacity for solitude, the state of rest and relaxation in an 'unintegrated state' is central. The unintegrated state is a state *away* from the formation of the ego. 'Not only are aspects of the baby felt as environment and aspects of the environment felt as self, but even where there is continuity in the line of life and moments of I AM the nascent self is not felt to be the same at all times' (Davis and Wallbridge, 1987: 34).

These moments of quietness, non-excitement and rest are moments of un-integration.

> in the quiet moments let us say that there is no line but lots of things that separate out, sky seen through trees, something to do with the mother's eyes all going in and out, wandering round. Some lack of need for any integration. That is an extremely valuable thing to be able to retain. Miss something without it. Something to do with being calm, restful relaxed and feeling one with people and things when no excitement is around. (cited in Davis and Wallbridge, 1987: 35)

However, gaining access to such solitude also means coming to terms with and recognising the 'primitive agonies', as Winnicott termed them, associated with fear of abandonment, isolation and neglect. These primitive agonies may be experienced as fears of going to pieces, of falling for ever, of there being complete isolation because there is no communication. 'Solitaries come to solidarity with the world especially in its brokenness alienation and poverty.' Being able to access this solitude as an adolescent and an adult requires practice. Youth work can offer access to such practice.

Key Terms

This chapter distinguishes between the experience of loneliness and the experience of solitude. **Solitude** is the capacity to be alone while retaining a sense of loving connection. It is intimately connected to **solidarity**, a sense of profound connectedness with others and with creation. For some this is connected with **spirituality** or **faith**.

Further Reading

Beckford, R. (2004) *God and the Gangs: An Urban Toolkit for Those Who Won't Be Bought Out, Sold Out or Scared Out.* London: DLT. Beckford gives an insight into the contribution the faith of the Black-led churches is making to young people's lives.

Dillard, A. (1975) *Pilgrim at Tinker Creek.* London: Picador. This work explores the power of being in nature as a source of education and as offering a sense of mystery.

Dowrick, S. (1992) *Intimacy and Solitude: Balancing Closeness and Independence.* London: The Women's Press. This offers practical resources for working with issues of solitude, isolation and loneliness.

Moss, B. (2005) *Religion and Spirituality.* Lyme Regis: Russell House. This usefully explores the difference between the two terms and argues a strong case for a spirituality in all practice.

15

Youth Work, Democracy and Participation

- Young people's participation is based on a recognition of rights and on an understanding of the importance of participatory citizenship in a democracy.
- Being clear how different levels of participation relate to power and where the powerful decisions which affect young people's lives are made is essential. These may not be at local level at all. The question of how participatory processes relate to democratically elected authorities is important, as are the dangers of rubber-stamping and tokenism.
- Neighbourhood mediation processes help build up young people's capacity to contribute to a wider political conversation.
- Processes of political education need to avoid the problem of 'manufactured voice'.
- Gaining a voice politically requires building alliances.

> I choose my language depending on which meeting I go into. So if it is a DFES meeting I say 'challenging', if it is Home Office I say 'enforcement', if it is Department of Health 'support' and to the Department of Communities I say 'empowering'. Honestly, you have to play the game across Whitehall. (Louise Casey in her own words: Society Guardian, 26 July 2006)

Louise Casey's ability to get things done, first as the 'Homelessness Tsar' then taking a lead on the Respect Agenda, was well recognised. Recognising which languages are legitimised in a particular Department of State and which are scorned is part of the politics of youth and community work. Discourses of active citizenship, democracy and participation offer a major source of legitimacy in youth work.

Participation and legitimation

A very significant change in the provision of services for young people, including the schools service, has been the extent to which young people's active participation is now sought in the context of shaping and developing services. The United Nations Convention on the Rights of the Child was ratified in the UK in 1991 and has had a significant impact on governments since. From 1997 in the UK most legislation affecting young people's services has required the active participation of children and young people in their delivery and implementation (Oldfield and Fowler, 2004).

Besides the major concern for advocacy for 'looked after children', a highly significant factor in the emergence and proliferation of invitations to participation has been the issue of the 'democratic deficit', by which is understood the declining participation in voting and support for political parties across the political spectrum. There is an understandable desire on the part of politicians to bring to an end this decline in political involvement. This is perceived as a Europe-wide issue:

> The active participation of young people in decisions and actions at local and regional levels is essential if we are to build more democratic, inclusive and prosperous societies. Participation in the democratic life of any community is about more than voting or standing in elections .... Participation and active citizenship is about having the right, the means, the space and the opportunity–and where necessary the support–to participate in and influence decisions and engage in actions and activities so as to contribute to building a better society. (Council of Europe, 2003)

Voluntary association, long seen as the hallmark of youth work, is increasingly recognised as a necessary feature of democratic civil society.

Participation in public decision-making. Participation and policy

So the inclusion of young people's voices is valued in the development of policies. Evidence of consultation with young people is increasingly required in the development and evaluation of services and is taken as a key indicator in relation to funding (Kirkby and Bryson, 2002).

Participation by children and young people takes a variety of forms: from the appointment of children's champions to the development of focus groups of young people who test out particular aspects of policy and practice such as Crime and Disorder or Healthy Schools, to the development of 'Shadow Boards', for example in the Connexions Service, which are made up entirely of a representative group of young people. The Hear by Right standards developed by the National Youth Agency and the Local Government Association were developed as a basis for evaluating young people's participation and involvement, and evaluation is a key moment in youth work processes.

There is no doubt that this policy direction is well intentioned and some distance removed from an alternative policy framework in which young people are responded to as objects of policy, as threatening or threatened youth. Nevertheless, there are a number of dangers associated with this strategy which have been summarised as 'ticking the boxes and missing the point'. It is as if young people are more and more involved in less and less. It is unclear to what extent the involvement of children and young people can enable them to determine the direction of strategies, policies and services, can enable them to set agendas rather than respond to them and it is unclear whether it would ever be thought right for them to do so.

In the absence of young people taking a strategic role there is a danger that their participation is required to give a veneer of democracy, simply to rubber-stamp or to fine-tune the direction of existing procedures.

Tokenism

There is also the danger of tokenism, the 'young person on the board' syndrome. Issues of democratic representation, of representativeness, of the fact that 'young people', like any other generational cohort, are not a homogeneous group: such issues arise regularly, and regularly create frustration. Although Shelley Arnstein's image of the 'ladder of participation' and its development by Roger Hart (1992) specifically for work with young people has now been critiqued considerably and is sometimes replaced by an account of 'participation pathways', this model has been widely used throughout community development practice since it was developed in 1969 to analyse forms of citizen action that were emerging at that time.

It is all too easy for issues of power to disappear within or beneath what are called the 'technologies' of participation, meaning the techniques and methods which have commonly been used. It is salutary to recognise that the first two steps on Arnstein's ladder are not actually steps of participation at all but should be understood as forms of disempowerment and manipulation. This critique has been voiced again very strongly in relation to young people's participation in focus groups and other 'technologies' of consultation. Where there is a great deal of consultation but very little devolved power the potential for disillusionment with democratic processes is great. The model of the ladder suggest that participation is best understood as moving 'vertically' or upwards towards the power holders/makers of public policy. However, participation has just as often been understood as mutual aid and self-help: the capacity to work together to get things done collectively at local level.

One of the most important tasks of the youth and community worker is to understand where the decisions are being taken that affect young people's lives, and this is likely to involve the worker in a global conversation as well as a very local one. It can be argued that ideas about 'community' and 'neighbourhood involvement' are no more than a very useful fiction for policy makers in a world in which key decisions are taken at the level of corporate boardrooms, not at local level at all.

Shelley Arnstein's ladder of participation (1969)

---

1. **Manipulation and 2. Therapy.** Both are non-participative. The aim is to cure or educate the participants. The proposed plan is best and the job of participation is to achieve public support by public relations.

3. **Informing.** A most important first step to legitimise participation. But too frequently the emphasis is on a one-way flow of information. No channel for feedback.

4. **Consultation.** Again a legitimate step–attitude surveys, neighbour-hood meetings and public inquiries. But Arnstein still feels this is just a window-dressing ritual.

5. **Placation.** For example, co-option of hand-picked 'worthies' on to committees. This allows citizens to advise or plan *ad infinitum* but retains for power holders the right to judge the legitimacy or feasibility of the advice.

6. **Partnership.** Power is in fact redistributed through negotiation between citizens and power holders. Planning and decision-making responsibilities are shared, e.g. through joint committees.

7. **Delegated power.** Citizens holding a clear majority of seats on committees with delegated powers to make decisions. Public now has the power to assure accountability of the programme to them.

8. **Citizen control.** Have-nots handle the entire job of planning, policy-making and managing a programme, e.g. neighbourhood corporation with no intermediaries between it and the source of funds.

Arnstein's ladder evolved in relation to models of citizen participation which were rooted in collective democratic traditions, traditions of strong trade unions able to exercise some collective influence on corporate power and a working representative democracy. The decline of the trade union movement and other forms of collective power which stood against the power of market-led forces has meant that notions of 'collectivity' are being re-invented.

Models of the collective voice are now also linked to the emergence of market research as a significant tool of government in the form of 'focus groups' for particular market segments, now refined to a level of postcode classifications. The renewed emphasis on the citizenship curriculum in schools and colleges has also opened up opportunities for the collective voice to be raised at a neighbourhood level. There are signs that trade unionism and other forms of workplace representation are beginning to re-emerge, providing a potentially global voice.

Citizenship education in schools embraces schools councils, youth councils and youth parliaments. The extent to which young people who have been socially excluded are able to be involved in such initiatives has been widely questioned. Once the initiatives have some success, however, it is likely that contradictions and tensions will emerge. The success of Newham Youth Parliament as a diverse network of young people elected by schools councils and other local youth forums has raised questions among the democratically elected councillors in the Borough and Local Authority which sponsors it.

The Scrutiny Report in Newham raised important questions about the Youth Parliament.

Discussion Point

'Is it a consultative group? A decision-making body? A provider of outreach and advocacy services for young people? Or is it an opportunity for young people involved in the Newham Youth Parliament to develop skills and to understand the value of engaging in the community?'

The issues of power and representativeness also emerge. 'In particular there needs to be a clear definition between the times when Newham Young People's Parliament is helping to develop policy and when it is implementing policy .... Some roles require a representative group and others may not.'

What powers should be delegated to unelected groups of young people?

In some places, these initiatives lack credibility among the young, because of their perceived lack of power. The question of 'what is within the scope' of such gatherings and 'what is outside their power' is critical. It seems in fact that there is a renewed emphasis on such shadow structures for young people in places where the derogated power of local authorities or regional assemblies is most circumscribed. As the powers of elected bodies have diminished, so the role of youth assemblies has become more visible.

However, well-organised expressions of 'Youth Voice' can offer significant power and therefore the possibility of change, and can enable youth workers and informal educators to break out of what are sometimes self-imposed ghettos of the local. Where youth forums can access financial resources–as was the case in Cheshire when the Youth Forum allocated half of the Youth Opportunities Fund to its representatives–young people may enter into democratic dialogue with some power behind them. In this case, the urgent issue of transport for young people in rural areas was to be negotiated and the representatives of Cheshire Youth Parliament had some £50,000 to offer to the process.

Participation and mediation

Another key area for public conversation involving young people is the arena of neighbourhood mediation. Young people can be collectively involved, with the support of informal educators, in community conferences designed to create bridges, for example between older and younger residents in communities as an alternative to the criminalisation and demonising of young people through the use of Anti-Social Behaviour Orders.

What is involved in mediation and what kinds of focus emerge in communities in which young people are perceived as at the centre of anti-social behaviour? This can involve a shared approach to conflict-mapping. Conflict-mapping is a systematic approach to conversation about the factors involved in a particular dispute or conflict. It asks questions such as:

- Who are the main parties involved in the conflict?
- What other parties are involved or connected in some way, including marginalised groups and external parties?
- What are the relationships between parties and how can they be represented?
- Who has alliances with whom?
- Who is in close contact with whom?
- Is there a history of broken relationships? Which are the broken relationships?
- Has confrontation happened? If so, what form is it taking?
- Are there any key issues between the parties that should be represented on the map?
- Where are you/your organisation in relation to these parties?

Once a conflict-mapping activity has taken place, it may be that members of the youth work team are able to act as mediators. Mediation involves all sides agreeing to participate and accept mediators. Mediators must be willing to work with all sides, and so need to set aside the youth work role of 'advocate for the young people'. They are looking not for an objective truth but for an agreed solution that takes into account the perceptions and experiences of all sides. The parties must all 'own' any agreement that is reached. Mediators usually work in pairs and use many of the same skills as informal educators, in particular the drawing up of ground rules, paraphrasing and summarising skills, and extensive capacity for empathy. They also need strategies for coping with strong emotions.

The mediation process is different from informal learning however in that it follows a structured pattern.

The Mediation Process

- Get agreement to embark on mediation.
- Make opening statements about the process, the ground rules and commitment to the process.
- Receive initial uninterrupted statements from each party.
- Clarify issues of disagreement and conflict.
- Agree agenda.
- Directly exchange needs and fears.
- Build acceptable alternatives.
- Finalise agreements.

Youth and community workers can themselves offer to act as mediators. More often they train young people to act as peer mediators and offer them support. In the case of mediation, there is a highly structured and formal conversation involved. There is a shift from informality to formality. There is also a shift of perspective to one that sits a little uneasily with the role of the youth worker. It involves a recognition that mediation requires an ability to be alongside both groups involved in a conflict rather than to take the side of the young people. However, such formal public conversation is sometimes an offshoot of informal conversation.

Imagine that a group of young people are congregating at a street corner, drinking in public, littering the area with empty beer cans. This is causing concern in the neighbourhood. Should the police be called? And what is the role of the youth and community worker at this point? It could be simply diversionary. Or it could involve mediation between particular groups of residents and young people, under the aegis of a community project. At this point, it becomes part of a wider set of social agendas and the youth worker can no longer be seen straightforwardly as 'on the side of the young people'. In order to act as a mediator, he/she must gain the trust of both sides and be prepared to listen to and acknowledge the perspectives and experiences of both sides.

Such mediation need not only reflect and respond to conflicts occurring at local level. It can involve the engagement with society-wide and global conflicts. This will be explored in the next chapter on community cohesion.

Manufactured voice: How is citizenship defined?

In all this it is important to recognise the significance of what has been termed 'manufactured voice'. This is created by a very tight control of political agendas followed by an invitation to join in a conversation. Only occasionally, and with devastating effect, does reality break in, as it did for New Labour under Tony Blair when, accused of not listening, the Prime Minister launched the 'Big Conversation'. When the Big Conversation website was filled with contributions protesting at the Government's involvement in war in Iraq, the website was closed down. Creating a framework for public conversation which means that public policy makers can only hear what they want to hear is not a framework for democratic renewal, and is justifiably treated with suspicion by youth and community workers. Local strategic partnerships have generated a strong elite consensus about the directions of cities, but they do quickly disarm opposition and deny space to any emerging alternative discourses.

It is far preferable that informal educators search out voices that are minoritised and marginalised in public conversations and seek, within the limits of an ethic of human rights and mutual care, to amplify them. Quite often, the democratic processes in which young people are engaged seek convergence and consensus. The question of what participatory democratic approaches are effective in working creatively with and even intensifying tension and conflict remains under-explored, although some new movements drawing on the traditions of citizen organising associated with Saul Alinsky are re-opening this issue (Chambers, 2003).

Underlying invitations to democracy are questions of power and control. Seeking young people's voice and point of view seems an obvious good. It is better than believing that children and young people should be 'seen and not heard'. However, the power differential between young people and adults, especially 'expert adults', is such that children's and young people's voices are easily discredited and ignored, even within systems which demand their 'participation'.

Too many calls for consultation and participation, especially in the fields of education, health and welfare, are based on existing constructions of the 'best interests' of young people and of poor communities. These constructions are facilitated, despite the rhetoric of collaboration and partnership, by a number of controlling strategies developed through the bureaucratic mandate of government. These include strategies such as criteria-setting, targeting through imposed initiatives and auditing. In 'deprived areas' cynicism about consultation initiatives and audit fatigue soon set in, not just among professionals but among young people and residents too. These initiatives and strategies are based on 'expert knowledge' about indicators of exclusion and deprivation, and it is in the context of such expertise that young people are invited to express their views, for example on the management of the Connexions office space for a young people's drop-in; or the nature of contraceptive advice locally; or the timing of counselling sessions for young people. In other words, the actual scope of young people's participation is limited by 'expert knowledges' which form the policy context. This means that the rhetoric of participation may still, in a wider context, deny young people voice. The construction of 'targets' and 'outcomes' effectively determines what can and cannot be voiced at any point, and the young person's participation as a 'target' for any given organisation takes precedence over any other directions for the conversation, especially those which suggest the Government is asking the wrong questions and seek to set a different agenda (Hodgson, 2004).

The view that participation in youth groups enhances democracy has its roots less in the practices of representation, consultation and policy-making that currently have centre stage and more in traditions that view associationalism and mutual aid, particularly through clubs and networks, as a buffer against totalitarianism. The experience of association and membership, of belonging, the experience of debate and of discussion and the development of shared purpose is what supports 'citizenship' rather than formal voting rights or patterns of representation. The ideal is of an informal self-organising self-help group based on trust and co-operative effort. Citizenship, in these terms, is concerned with participation in civil society as a good in itself. Rather than being based on the acquisition of rights to influence it is rooted in the development of a network of mutual connection. As John Bamber put it, in an important critical reflection on notions of active citizenship undertaken at the beginning of the New Labour period:

Discussion Point

There is a danger of over emphasising youth work as a means of delivering 'capable' young people into the worlds of work and training and other current social agendas .... Youth workers can contribute to the work of other agencies in cross-disciplinary settings, since there are certain aspects of the methodology and process which are transferable. What may be described as mainstream youth work, however, has its own distinctive purpose, which is to engage with young people in situations and on terms over which they have some control. This is why voluntary association and the informal approach are so important and cannot be separated from mainstream youth work. (John Bamber, 2002)

How do youth workers promote opportunities for association where young people start the agenda, when funding is so heavily targeted?

Bamber's model of educational groupwork moves from 'articulating propositions' to 'developing knowledge' to 'taking action'. The movement from 'competitive assertion' to 'collaborative enquiry' is the characteristic movement of informal learning processes. This collaborative enquiry then leads to a desire for collective action. Such a process of education lends itself to democratic renewal. It is the obverse of focus groups when the agenda is set by policy makers or by market researchers.

Citizenship and alliance-building

The idealisation of civil society as the place in which 'social capital' is being created forms a strong current of New Labour thinking. The tensions, conflicts and problems which beset the 'third sector' (the community and voluntary sector) are denied in such idealisations. Specifically, the issue of how groups which are marginalised in current structures develop and gain power and recognition is not addressed (Young, 2000).

The 'belonging' engendered in civil society and the 'bonding' aspect so beloved by theorists of social capital has little to say, for example, about the struggles of the voluntary sector, of the Black and minority ethnic sector, of the struggles facing disabled people's organisations or the development of lesbian, gay, bisexual and trans community organisations. Not only do these communities of interest struggle to create collective voice, but their young people are often marginalised within them. In each case in order to sustain young people's interests within emerging community organisations, it has been necessary both to emphasise community development activities and to develop separate provision for young people's groups.

Alliances have been necessary in the attempt to develop public conversation on the part of historically marginalised groups. Sometimes there has been a strong emphasis on the importance of separation and a recognition of the specific interests of particular groups. At other times there has been a deliberate construction of alliances. The example of 'Broad Based Organising' as a method which brings together an alliance which is large and strong enough to bring pressure to bear on corporate power is an instructive one here. 'Broad Based Organising' developed in the United States from the work of the Citizen Organising Foundation and has emerged with particular strength in the UK in East London, developing leaders and offering collective affiliations to large local 'civil society' organisations which then combine to pursue specific campaigns, such as the 'Living Wage' campaigns designed to raise the wages of the lowest-paid employees in major workplaces in the area affected by the citizens' organisation, most notably TELCO in East London, in alliance with London citizens (Pierson, and Smith, 2001).

Young people too must be given opportunities for conversation in settings that affirm otherwise marginalised and discredited aspects of identity: such as lesbian, gay, bisexual and transgender groups; or disabled people's groups. They benefit from collective strength, in the context of alliance and in the recognition of autonomy (Ledwith and Asgill, 2000). People have multiple identifications, but at every point when a power struggle is engaged, certain of those identifications come to the fore. Others will be positioned as 'allies' or 'supporters'. Youth and community workers will always need to ask 'Who are the allies of the young people? Who is fighting for their particular interests?'

The need to seek common ground and to establish the basis of alliances has been a principle behind much creative practice in recent years. Alliances can never be entirely predicted and the relationship between commonality and difference is never 'sorted' once and for all. Yet by the development of alliances within the public life of a city or conurbation, power can be shared and extended at an individual, group and organisational level.

We need models of democracy that move beyond the rational and deliberative. Democracy as struggle and contestation needs to develop new forms. Perhaps it is only if democracy can be understood again as a vehicle for struggling over the allocation of resources that we will shift a pattern in which young people in the UK (the fourth-richest nation in the world) are encouraged to participate more than they have ever been and yet are found to be, according to the 2007 UNICEF report, alongside children from the United States, the worst off materially and emotionally of the children of any nation of the developed world (UNICEF, 2007).

Key Terms

Participation means more than simply 'taking part'. It refers to young people's rights to have a say in ways that make a difference in decisions that affect their lives.

Community development is grounded in self-identified needs, self-help and mutual aid. It offers a strong basis for young people's participation.

Citizenship education is based on collaborative enquiry into current realities of young people's lives, including current political realities. Citizenship means political, social, economic and sexual participation in the life of the society, and enables the exercise of rights.

Further Reading

Badham, B. (2004) *Act by Right*. Leicester: National Youth Agency. This text offers a widely recognised basis for evaluating young people's participation.

Chambers, E. (2003) *Roots for Radicals: Organizing for Power, Action and Justice*. New York and London: Continuum. This text shows a way of renewing citizen action based on Alinsky's work.

Pierson, J. and Smith, J. (2001) *Rebuilding Communities: Common Problems and Approaches*. Basingstoke: Palgrave. This text explores many debates about participation in regeneration.

16

Community Cohesion and Transversal Politics

- 'Community Cohesion' is a complex and contradictory agenda for youth work to address. It contains celebration, calls for public order and surveillance and a denial of persistent inequality.
- A number of methods of work that have been developed globally in the context of conflict can be drawn on. These methods work outwards from the immediate and local and are unafraid of engaging with difference as conflict.
- Youth work using sport; local memory/local history and intergenerational work promotes community cohesion.
- The idea of 'transversal politics' – crossing conflict zones – offers an alternative framework to more limited models of multiculturalism. Examples of anti-racist practice, of anti-sectarian work, and of peace processes and Truth and Reconciliation processes are given.
- The question of what new models of democratic connection might replace the concept of 'community cohesion' is raised.

The desire for conversation with new people, for new conversations – not just the same old 'family' or 'in-group' conversation–the opportunities provided by urban living for 'being together with strangers': these are some of the desires and opportunities that are harnessed when youth and community workers are engaged in strategies which promote 'community cohesion'.

In the summer of 2001 disturbances took place in the English towns of Oldham, Burnley, Bradford, Leeds and Stoke-on-Trent. The disturbances were apparently racially inspired and occurred between largely Asian and largely white working-class neighbourhoods. Following the Bradford riots, a ministerial review group reported (Denham, 2002) as well as an independent community cohesion review team under Ted Cantle (Cantle, 2001). The extent to which speaking about 'communities' rapidly replaced a political agenda which had increasingly focused on challenging institutional racism – after the McPherson Inquiry (1999) into the killing of Stephen Lawrence, and the Race Relations (Amendment) Act (2000) – is remarkable. Following the disturbances it was immediately recognised by the exponents of youth work that they had much to offer to the policies and strategies outlined in the reports that followed (Thomas, 2003).

The theoretical underpinnings of the approach to community cohesion draws on models of social cohesion and social capital (Field, 2003) which describe and seek

- common values and a civic culture
- social order and social control
- social solidarity and reductions in wealth disparities
- social networks and social capital
- place, attachment and identity

With ever more intensity following the attacks on the World Trade Center and the subsequent period of the 'War on Terror' – including the 7 July 2006 attacks in London – the calls to combat segregation in the name of cohesion have been repeated. Sometimes 'community cohesion' seems to be a strategy for integration. At other moments it seems to be a strategy largely concerned with preserving public order.

In this context, youth workers may find themselves working not only in support of young people but on behalf of an idealised image of a 'multicultural nation' in which everyone has learned to 'celebrate the difference'. They may also be called on to offer this celebration in an affirmation of 'belonging to Britain', whatever the material inequalities and patterns of exclusion with which young people are faced. This context is immensely paradoxical and poses many dilemmas and challenges (Ahmed, 2004).

The question of 'them' and 'us': local identifications and belonging

Critical educational practices can begin to explore and resist the dominant constructions of 'them' and 'us' by enabling the exploration of common ground and difference in new and less stereotypical ways. In such practice, it is useful to recognise both the potential and the dangers of the discourse of 'community cohesion'.

Youth and community work has always started with 'local conversations', and the potential to link the local with the global is one of the great strengths of the practice of informal learning: often this results from the interests and enthusiasms of young people.

Sport as a vehicle for cross-community bonding

The Unity Cup brought together 20 teams from refugee and asylum-seeking communities to highlight the positive contribution of asylum seekers and to counter negative stereotypes. The Sheffield-based Football Unites, Racism Divides has strong links with local youth work.

The significance of football in those Northern towns which have been the focus of the 'community cohesion' initiatives is inestimable. The Football Museum and the Youth and Community Service in Preston have been the focus of a number of recent initiatives including a project in Deepdale, Preston which involved local young Asian women in making a film about the importance of football in their community. In Burnley, outreach work between Burnley FC and teams from local Asian leagues has offered opportunities to play football in shared leagues and mixed teams.

Such local initiatives make a strong basis for national campaigns, the most significant of which is Let's Kick Racism out of Football. Let's Kick Racism out of Football is a rolling programme of events supported by the Football Association and the Commission for Racial Equality which challenges racism and supports footballers from minority ethnic communities acting as positive role models to young people. This contributes to the process of disentangling 'Englishness' from an exclusive 'colouring' of 'whiteness'. The link between sport and national identities is of importance in challenging racism, as the national teams are clearly teams made up of players of a variety of heritages and skin tones within the nation.

However, nationalism in sport can also be a powerful intensifier of exclusionary practices. Not everything always goes smoothly. Fiercely fought football games often raise questions for youth work practitioners about the impact of competitive play and how it is handled so that it does not merely entrench division along racialised or, in the case of refugee teams, war-zone lines. Youth work strategies which emphasise city or even neighbourhood pride rather than national pride are valuable in promoting new senses of belonging. Local teams, which are often very much loved by their supporters, continue to have an important part to play in conveying something about the loyalties and sense of 'inclusion' and 'exclusion' which their supporters share.

Local/global journeys: roots and routes

Local history and local roots projects have enabled the re-imagining of neighbourhoods and their histories. The period of the Second World War has often been seen as a uniquely positive moment in a sense of shared national identity. Everyone – not only the servicemen and their families – was affected by that war, by the air raids and the rationing and the evacuations. When young people involved in youth work in Blackburn interviewed local Second World War veterans from the Asian communities, they not only undertook significant inter-generational work in their own communities. They also challenged the 'whitening' of images and memories of the nation pulling together in common cause, and widened the definition both of the shared identity and the 'common ground'. They prevented the complete writing out of the presence and participation of those 'other' communities during the war and therefore of an important aspect of twentieth-century history of the British as a cosmopolitan and hybrid people (Hall, 2000). The support which cotton workers and their families gave to the Indian resistance struggle and the significance of 'Mr Gandhi's' visit to Blackburn also has a place of honour and is a source of pride in local history.

The history of Moss Side in Manchester, like that of other neighbourhoods which welcomed, however ambivalently, post-war migrants, is also currently being retold. The retelling of recent history provides an important alternative focus for informal education in a community which becomes invisible except at times of shootings and gang crime (John, 2006). The community's struggles over housing and the fact that the first arrivals from Jamaica to Moss Side were largely owner-occupiers has been written out of the history of the redevelopment of Manchester. This redevelopment has left the grandchildren of those first migrants largely in social housing in one or two local estates. This history is now being retold for the benefit of young people who know nothing of it and yet see continuous representations of gun- and gang-related crime in their areas of the city.

Similarly, young people in Burnley who are involved with 'Building Bridges Burnley' report the powerful effect on them of the media representations of Burnley as synonymous with the British National Party, rather than for example with their own creative efforts at community-building. The 'amplification' through the media of these alternative histories is very important and youth workers engaging in such work need to build good links with the local and national press, radio and TV.

In contemporary migrations, the old colonial and missionary journeys undertaken by the British are now being trodden in a reverse direction. 'Just Youth' in Salford was established by Nigerian priests to offer a service and a justice-and-peace based education programme to schools in the Roman Catholic Diocese of Salford. New waves of migrants, who are refugees and asylum seekers, as well as economic migrants, are supported by local informal education projects. Saying Power, a West London based project working with refugees and asylum seekers, offers seven hours a week of individual mentor support, as well as groupwork, on the basis of which young people meet in mixed or culturally specific groups to design their own projects and initiatives.

Transversal politics: crossing conflict zones

The contemporary journeys, visits and exchanges which form part of youth and community work are important in the development of what has been called 'transversal politics'. This is a way of describing the border crossings in which people come together peacefully to explore conflict zones; it happens in residentials, on international exchanges and visits, and in music workshops as well as more explicitly in youth work associated with peace processes in Belfast; or in women's inter-faith journeys.

Such initiatives sometimes provide an intense and life-changing experience; they may also provide a space for dislodging of stereotypes and for new learning about self and others. They unsettle existing accounts of 'difference' and make it difficult to reproduce accounts of experience as either 'monocultural' or 'multicultural'. It is important that informal educators seek out conversations which unsettle our perceptions of these 'realities' of difference, which in fact are continually constructed and amplified through processes of repetition and normalisation across society so that we all come to believe that we 'know' rather than need to discover where, if anywhere, our differences lie. In this context, youth workers need to enable resistance to the discourse that constructs white working-class people living on estates as uniformly racist. Connections and solidarity emerge out of 'rubbing along together' and sharing common ground, having aspects of life in common, rather than from ritualised performance of 'exotic' differences of the 'steel bands and samosas' variety (Chauhan, 1989).

The multiculturalism of the kind which was practised in the 1980s tended to be backward looking in its construction of 'culture' rather than imagining a future which is producing new connections and combinations: the fast food 'curry and chips' and 'halal pizzas' of British cities. Emphasising cultural difference in the context of powerful political and ideological divides, such as those generated during war, always risks playing to the most 'backward looking' and reified aspects of cultural formations. In the future-oriented inter-cultural conversations in which informal educators are engaging, roots are being replaced by routes and journeys (Gilroy, 1993).

Peace processes

Truth and reconciliation

In some contexts, the experience of conflict has been so intense and prolonged that communities are now engaged in a deliberate 'peace process' in which the past is confronted in the present. Without such a process it is reckoned that there will be no possibility of a more open future or of preventing the recurrence of violence. The chief model for such a peace process is drawn from the work of the Truth and Reconciliation Commission as it has been developed in South Africa.

It is important that this process is not a court of law, and this gives rise to a great deal of debate. In particular Truth and Reconciliation processes have to address the charge that in promoting peace they avoid the issue of justice.

The elements of the Truth and Reconciliation Commission's process have been described as concerned with different levels of truth. Truth is factual and the hearing of true stories matters: it provides evidential knowledge and acknowledgement of who did what and when. Many histories of conflict and violence involve a set of rumours and counter-rumours and myths about how particular episodes of conflict began. Factual truth has a very powerful role to play in the dispelling of such rumours.

Truth also has a narrative form. It involves stories with characters and plot lines and significant events full of meaning for the people involved. Telling and circulating truthful stories enables people to make sense of their lives in new ways. To be able to tell a story which makes sense is an important part of the recovery from apparently senseless violence and conflict.

Truth is social. It is not a private matter but has a resonance within communities. In this way it contributes not only to a personal story but to public stories and versions of events.

Finally, truth is healing. The ability to tell stories which make sense and which do not have gaps in them is a very important factor in recovery from the hurt and damage that conflict creates. It can slow down the process or even change the direction of the process through which revenge is sought. In this sense truth-telling contributes to the possibility of wholeness and healing for both perpetrators and victims of violence. It opens up the possibility of reconciliation between warring communities and groups.

Recognition is significant. This involves the recognition of one's enemy as a human being, for who he or she is. This opens up the possibility of contrition and forgiveness. Memories are invoked and spoken rather than left silent, thereby creating the possibility of healing. And surprises are anticipated. New aspects of a situation are discovered and learned.

Conflict mediation

Community cohesion projects invariably confront the realities of both segregation and racism in particular localities and it is therefore necessary to identify and develop project work which recognises the nature of the conflicts and does not evade them. Anti-racist and anti-sectarian work is not 'one off' but needs to be committed to over a significant period of time, if it is to contribute to shifting an existing culture in particular neighbourhoods. Youth and community worker's commitment to challenge verbal expressions of racism is an important one which is easily trivialised, just as, in general, the distress to children and young people caused by name-calling is easily trivialised by adults. Yet it has been well established that racist insults are the most frequently experienced form of racial abuse and harassment, existing at one end of a continuum of harassment, with assault, gang attacks and even murder at the other.

Anti-racist practice

One of the fullest existing accounts of detached youth work which explores in detail the processes of anti-racist informal education is to be found in Stella Dadzie's *Blood, Sweat and Tears* (1997), an account of the work of the Bede Detached Work project in Bermondsey. The Bede Detached Work project made a commitment always to challenge racist comments and intimidating behaviour, a commitment which was rooted in a practice of valuing and respecting young people and being able to distinguish between the young person and their behaviour.

Challenging racism took the form of direct or indirect, premeditated or spontaneous, responses to whatever came up in their conversations. Humour played an important part, as did the workers' individual life experiences – which included knowledge of the National Front and The British National Party; experience of growing up as a Black man in the East End of London which provided the team with detailed knowledge of drugs and other issues; and fifteen years of working with young people, including a project in Belfast.

One of the difficulties of positive action strategies as a means of combating discrimination is that, in seeking to create fairness for a particular highlighted group – be it the Somalis, the Bangladeshis, the Pakistanis, the Jamaicans – a sense of envy among other groups who share the same neighbourhood is frequently activated.

One of the most powerful forms racism takes is a false sense of injustice which masks the real injustice of a particular situation. This sense of 'unfairness' is often articulated in terms of a racialised 'them' and 'us' – 'they get their voices heard; they get more (housing ... jobs ... trips ... sessions ...) than us whites' (Dadzie, 1997).

The sense of unfairness is a powerful screen to a full understanding of the nature and meaning of racism. Some anti-racist initiatives can in their turn pathologise white working-class communities, producing a sense either that they are the only ethnic group *without* a culture or that their culture is nothing but pure negativity.

Yet the injustices that young people in poor neighbourhoods face are real enough and are usually shared across all communities in those neighbourhoods. They are largely the responsibility of forces and groups entirely external to that neighbourhood.

Case Study

The willingness to address all aspects of young people's experience was important since their racism could not be separated from the many other problems they were facing. Alcohol and drug use, petty crime, truancy, school exclusions, joblessness, homelessness and diffi-culties with parents also featured prominently in many young people's lives and it was by addressing these issues that the team was able to gain their trust and confidence. The team's agreed approach was to explore with them how little they had to gain from blaming black people for a political situation that ordinary people were not responsible for. (Dadzie, 1997)

Truly transformative cultural initiatives are to be found in the creative tension between a practice which does not avoid racism and a practice which listens, stays in there and does not condemn. All this takes time, and time is all too often in short supply where projects are conceived on too short term a basis. The conversations of detached youth work projects are interventions into networks; they may well focus on key individuals, such as gang leaders, but they do this in order to bring about new conversations in a network, drawing on a peer dynamic to facilitate peer edu-cation. The length of time that projects can be funded for tends to result in 'one-off' events of limited value. What is needed is a long view, work over at least three years.

Cross-community practice and peace process

The experience of cross-community work in the Northern Ireland Youth Service also provides a resource for deepening understanding of community cohesion initiatives. The Northern Ireland Youth Service contribution to the peace process is named JEDI – the 'J', 'was added as a weak attempt at humour which stuck', – standing for Joined Together. E–D–I stand for Equity, Diversity and Interdependence. These are the values which underpin the peace process work being developed by informal educators. These values are explored in all the activities the Northern Ireland Youth Service supports. The Kairos Project, developed by Northern Ireland Youthlink, is a resource for peacemakers. *Kairos* is a Greek word for a 'special time, God's time' and the resource was developed with local church and community youth groups to 'guide young people on a journey to be creative peacemakers in our divided society'.

Case Study

Kairos, Northern Ireland Youthlink

The process begins with what is named 'single identity work'. That is, it begins where young people are and with their identification with a specific cultural identity. The strengths and positive aspects of this identity are explored, in their own right and not as defined by or for others, certainly not as defined against others.

It is in this context that the possibility of and positive reasons for making contact with young people whose communities have historically been defined as 'enemies' can be explored. The second stage of the Kairos process is a 'contact event' through which young people learn something of one another's lives and stories. Out of this contact, shared work on a practical project is developed. So this leads to a third stage, which is a contribution to the renewal of a particular community and the building up of cross-community resources for the future.

The story-telling aspect of this work is crucial. People's personal stories can be transformative and empowering in the process of change.

Like the anti-racist practice in the Bede Detached Work project, the Kairos project depends on a positive non-judgmental approach alongside a commitment to counter prejudicial speech and threatening behaviour. Given that religion is often represented as a key axis of conflict, the importance of drawing on faith-based resources which facilitate bridge-building cannot be overestimated. The image of the journey and of life as a journey as well as learning as a journey has become something of a cliché, yet it is an image of powerful cultural significance to many migrant peoples as well as in the faiths which begin with the nomad Abraham. How do journeying and conversation interconnect?

Case Study

The Henry Martyn Foundation has developed a methodology of women's inter-faith journeys. They began when a team of nine women (four Indians, four Canadians and a facilitator) travelled together for a period of seven weeks, in India first for three and a half weeks and then nine months later in Canada for three and a half weeks. During the journey they told the stories of their own lives as mothers, daughters, sisters and friends. They did not talk *about* inter-faith but instead connected in a holistic way, allowing their life narratives to become entangled and connected rather than offering key concepts for debate. The journeying methodology creates a need for exploration of self as well as of belief and concepts.

Like many inter-cultural projects that have been developed out of the Canadian experience, women's inter-faith journeys make use of the talking circle or pow-wow derived from Native American context. The pow-wow involves listening, discerning, finding direction, becoming centred in a group. Out of this initial journey, women's inter-faith journeys have developed as a methodology for addressing conflict. The objectives of the projects are to identify from women's perspective the underlying issues in existing conflicts; to discern the contribution of religious and spiritual identities to such conflicts, and to explore alternative models of peace-building that arise out of women's experience.

Community cohesion?

Analysis of the discourses of community cohesion raises a set of complex issues. Informal education has been theorised as building up the social capital needed for regeneration and for community cohesion. In particular, there has been an emphasis on the capacity of informal education to undertake the 'bridging' and 'linking' work needed to facilitate social integration.

Political exclusion is rarely discussed in the surveys of social exclusion. Indicators on such matters as voting levels, membership of political parties, community participation, and membership of trade unions or tenant's associations are rarely produced as significant indicators of social exclusion. Yet community cohesion is at least as much a political as a neighbourhood priority.

It is important to stress once more the danger of 'manufactured voice' (Hodgson, 2004). Systems for 'linking' are easily designed which ensure that the powerful, particularly politicians and policy makers, hear only what they want to hear. Models of community cohesion, rooted as they are in images of social integration, tend to seek and promote consensus and a recognition of commonality. Although the rhetoric of 'celebrating differences' is often present there are few forums which make this possible on a sustained basis, so differences which embody real conflicts of interest are unlikely to be aired. The notion of 'young people's voice' is important but it needs to be deconstructed. Practices associated with 'active citizenship' and 'community cohesion' need to begin with plurality, the recognition that young people are as likely as adults to be diverse and divergent in their voices. Otherwise integration will always be promoted on the terms of the dominant group and 'community cohesion' will become another version of 'assimilation'.

The socialist-feminist writer Donna Haraway's image of an 'infidel heteroglossia' is suggestive and at the same time almost impossible to pin down (Haraway, 1991a). It is a deliberately irreverent image of 'speaking with many tongues', speaking in many languages and talking about everything imaginable, and then imagining talking about things that it might seem unimaginable to talk about at present. It suggests a way of dreaming about a politics adequate to the representation of our multiplicities and our wildest dreams as well as of our common ground.

In any democratic forum or any 'inter-cultural' work there will only be partial connection, but there nevertheless needs to be a commitment to communication between all the parts of the whole. Communication will not happen naturally, organically, because they 'are all young people' or 'they are all clients/service users' or 'we have a neutral venue', although all these things help. Those who construct such boundaries and bridges and establish new forums and neutral venues to promote community cohesion have a responsibility also to think through and create the new possibilities for communication and conversation, and need to be prepared to be very amazed and unsettled by what emerges.

Such new processes of communication involve both anger and love. They involve the destruction of identities and categories that discourses of social exclusion and community cohesion take as natural and for granted. They involve the recognition of the provisionality of all identities and the construction of new identities and communites more open to change, networked rather than gated communities, places for as yet unimagined and unfinished conversations.

This chapter has explored the difficulties and potential of discourses of 'community cohesion' for youth work. It has highlighted some well established methods of informal learning which enable new conversations to emerge. The creation of spaces in which they can continue has also been highlighted, as a work undertaken, often in anger and, very often, in surprise and love.

Key Terms

The idea of **transversal politics** includes ideas about crossing borders and also about building bridges. It is a form of politics associated with peace processes in a time of conflict, recognising power struggles without necessarily joining them.

Further Reading

Dadzie, S. (1997) *Blood, Sweat and Tears.* Leicester: Youth Work Press.
Hall, S. (2000) 'Conclusion: the multicultural question', in Hannibal-Paci, C. (2002) *Un/settled Multiculturalisms: Diasporas, Entanglements, Transruptions.* Durham, NC: Duke University Press.
Wilson, R. (2006) *What Works for Reconciliation?* Belfast: Democratic Dialogue.

Each of these texts moves the thinking about diversity out of a static multiculturalism and into a sense of the transformative power of challenging injustice and working with a sense of movement and creativity in cultures which embrace difference rather than commodify it.

Part IV

Unfinished Conversations
Reflection Points

- Do you notice the times when young people are silent? What is the meaning of their silences?
- How do you establish an anti-bullying culture in your practice? Where does the practice of mediation appear in your work? At an interpersonal level? At community level? In relation to major conflicts or histories of war?
- How do you respond to signs of anger or distress in a young person?
- How do the young people you are working with understand risk and risk-taking?
- What resources does your youth work have to offer a young person who has attempted suicide? What resources does your youth work have to offer young people who have experienced the death of someone close to them?
- What are the opportunities you offer to young people to experience a sense of joy, awe and wonder? How do you engage young people in an appreciation of the natural world and of wilderness places?
- Do you use the resources of residentials, retreats or journeys in your practice, and what is the rationale for them?
- How do the young people you work with develop a sense of belonging? How do they develop a sense of connection with others, locally and globally?
- Do young people with whom you work know about opportunities to participate in public decision-making and have a voice? How do you support them to take up these opportunities?
- In relation to what you believe people have in common and what you believe are the meanings associated with 'difference', are you prepared to be surprised?

References

Adams, J. (2007) *Go Girls! Supporting Girls' Emotional Development and Building Self-esteem*. Brighton: TSA.

Ahmed, S. (2004) *The Cultural Politics of Emotion*. Edinburgh: Edinburgh University Press.

Allport, G. (1954) *The Nature of Prejudice*. Reading, MA: Addison-Wesley.

Anthias, F. and Yuval Davis, M. (1992) *Racialised Boundaries: Race, Gender, Colour and Class in the Anti-Racist Struggle*. London: Routledge.

Archard, D. (2004) *Children: Rights and Childhood*. London: Routledge.

Arnstein, S. (1969) 'A ladder of citizen participation in the USA', *Journal of American Institute of Planners*, 35 (4): 216–24.

Back, L. (1996) *New Ethnicities and Urban Culture: Racism and Multiculture in Young Lives*. London: UCL Press.

Badham, B. (2004) *Act by Right*. Leicester: National Youth Agency.

Bamber, J. (2002) 'Educational groupwork and active citizenship: towards a theoretical framework', *Youth and Policy* 74: 1–17.

Banks, S. (ed.)(1999) *Ethical Issues in Youth Work*. London: Routledge.

Barry, M. (ed.) (2006) *Youth Policy and Social Inclusion: Critical Debate with Young People*. London: Routledge.

Batsleer, J. (1996) *Working with Girls and Young Women in Community Settings*. Ashgate: Arena.

Batsleer, J. (2003) 'Practices of friendship', in Gilchrist, R., Jeffs, T. and Spence, J. (eds), *Architects of Change: Studies in the History of Community and Youth Work*. Leicester: National Youth Agency.

Beckford, R. (2004) *God and the Gangs: An Urban Toolkit for Those Who Won't Be Bought Out, Sold Out or Scared Out*. London: DLT.

Ben-Ari, A. and Gil, S. (1998) 'Perceptions of life and death among suicidal gay adolescents', *Omega, Journal of Death and Dying*, 37(2): 107–18.

Bennett, A. (2000) *Popular Music and Youth Culture: Music Identity and Place*. Basingstoke: Macmillan.

Bennett, A. and Kahn-Harris, K. (eds) (2004) *After Sub-Culture: Critical Studies in Contemporary Youth Culture*. Basingstoke: Palgrave Macmillan.

Bhaba, H. and Gilman, S. (2001) 'Just talking: tête à tête', in Salamensky, S. I. (ed.), *Talk, Talk, Talk: The Cultural Life of Everyday Conversation*. London: Routledge.

Blake, S. and Brown, R. (2007) *Boys' Own: Supporting Self-esteem and Emotional Resourcefulness*. Brighton: TSA.

Boal, A. (1992) *Games for Actors and Non-Actors*. London: Routledge.

Boal, A. (1998) *The Legislative Theatre Using Performance to Make Politics*. London: Routledge.

Boal, A. (2000) *Theatre of the Oppressed*. London: Pluto Press.

Borden, I. (1998) 'An affirmation of urban life: skateboarding and socio-spatial censorship in the late twentieth century city', *ARCHIS*, 1998(5).

Borden, I. (2001) *Skateboarding, Space and the City: Architecture and the Body.* New York: Berg.

Bradshaw, J. et al. (2004) *The Drivers of Social Exclusion.* London: Social Exclusion Unit Office of the Deputy Prime Minister.

Brent, J. (2004) 'Communicating what youth work achieves: the Smile and the Arch', *Youth and Policy*, 84: 69–73.

Bridge, G. and Watson, S. (2003) *A Companion to the City.* Oxford: Blackwell.

Bynner, J. and Parsons, S. (2001) 'Qualifications, basic skills and accelerating social exclusion', *Journal of Education and Work*, 14(3): 279–91.

Cameron, D. and Kulick, D. (2003) *Language and Sexuality.* Cambridge: CUP.

Cantle, T. (2001) *Community Cohesion: A Report of the Review Team.* London: Home Office.

Carpenter, V. and Young, K. (1986) *Coming in from the Margins. Youth Work with Girls and Young Women.* Leicester: National Association of Youth Clubs.

Cass, V. C. (1979) 'Homosexual identity formation: a theoretical model', *Journal of Homosexuality*, 4(3): 219–35.

Catan, L. (2004) *Becoming Adult: Changing Youth Transitions in the 21st Century.* Brighton: Trust for the Study of Adolescence.

Chambers, E. (2003) *Roots for Radicals: Organizing for Power, Action and Justice.* New York and London: Continuum.

Chauhan, V. (1989) *Beyond Steel Bands and Samosas: Black Young People in the Youth Service.* Leicester: National Youth Bureau, Commission for Racial Equality.

Chauhan, V. (2003) 'Revolutionising youth work: black perspectives in global youth work', *Youth and Policy*, 80: 34–44.

Cohen, P. (1997) *Rethinking the Youth Question.* London: Routledge.

Cohen, P. (1990) *Really Useful Knowledge? Photography and Cultural Studies in Pre-Vocational Education.* London: Trentham.

Cohen, S. (1972) *Folk Devils and Moral Panics.* Oxford: Blackwell.

Coles, B. (2005) 'Youth policy 1995–2005: From "the Best Start" to "Youth Smatters"', *Youth and Policy*, 89, Autumn: 7–26.

Collander Brown, D. (2005) 'Being with another as a professional practitioner', *Youth and Policy*, 86, Winter: 33–47.

Colley, H. (2003) *Mentoring for Social Inclusion: A Critical Approach to Nurturing Mentor Relationships.* Falmer and London. Routledge.

Colley, H. and Hodkinson, P. (2001) 'Problems with bridging the gap: The reversal of structure and agency in addressing school exclusion', *Critical Social Policy*, 21(3): 335–59.

Condor, S. (2006) 'Public prejudice as collaborative accomplishment: towards a dialogic social psychology of racism', *Journal of Community and Applied Social Psychology*, 16: 1–18.

Cowie, H. and Wallace, P. (2000) *Peer Support in Action: From Bystanding to Standing By.* London: Sage.

Crimmens, D. and Whalen, A. (1999) 'Rights-Based Approaches to Work with Young People', in Banks, S. (ed.), *Ethical Issues in Youth Work.* London: Routledge.

Cross, W.E. (1980) 'Models of psychological nigrescence. A literature review', in Jones R.L. (ed.), *Black Psychology.* New York: Harper & Row.

Dadzie, S. (1997) *Blood, Sweat and Tears.* Leicester: Youth Work Press.

Davies, B. (1999) *A History of the Youth Service in England Vol. 1 1939–1979. From Voluntaryism to Welfare.* Leicester: Youth Work Press.

Davies, B. (2000) *Streetcred? Values and Dilemmas in Mental Health Work with Young People.* Manchester: 42nd Street.

Davies, B. (2005) *Youth Work: A Manifesto for Our Times.* Leicester: National Youth Agency.

Davies, D. (1995) *Pink Therapy: A Guide for Working with Lesbian, Gay and Bisexual Clients.* London: Open University Press.

Davis, M. and Wallbridge, D. (1987) *Boundary and Space: An Introduction to the Work of D.W. Winnicott*. London and New York: Brunner-Routledge.

Dean, J. (1996) *Solidarity of Strangers. Feminism after Identity Politics*. Berkeley: University of California Press.

Delgado, R. (2001) *Critical Race Theory: An Introduction*. New York: New York University Press.

Denham, J. (2002) *Building Cohesive Communities: A Report of the Ministerial Review Group on Public Order and Community Cohesion*. London: Home Office.

Department of Education and Science (1991) *Youth Work with Young People with Disabilities: A Report by HMI*. London: DES.

Department of Health (2004) *Teenage Parents: Who Cares?* London: DOH Teenage Pregnancy Unit.

Development Education Association (2004) *Global Youth Work Training and Practice Manual*. London: DEA.

Dillard, A (1975) *Pilgrim at Tinker Creek*. London: Picador.

Dowrick, S. (1992) *Intimacy and Solitude: Balancing Closeness and Independence*. London: The Women's Press.

Erikson, E.H. (1968) *Identity, Youth and Crisis*. New York: Norton.

Factor, F. Chauhan, V. and Pitts, J. (2001) *The RHP Companion to Working with Young People*. Lyme Regis: Russell House.

Fahmy, E. (2005) 'Youth, poverty and social exclusion', in Gordon, D., Levitas, R. and Pantazis, C. (eds), *Poverty and Social Exclusion in Britain: The Millennium Survey*. Bristol: Policy Press. pp. 347–73.

Fanon, F. (1986) *Black Skins, White Masks*. London: Pluto Press.

Field, J. (2003) *Social Capital*. London: Routledge.

Fine, N. and Macbeth, F. (1992) *Playing with Fire: Training in the Creative Use of Conflict*. Leicester: National Youth Agency.

42nd Street (2005) *Not Exactly Congratulations: Exploring the Emotional Wellbeing of Teenage Mothers and the Relevance of Postnatal Depression*. Manchester: 42nd Street.

Fraser, N. (1995) 'From redistribution to recognition: dilemmas of justice in a post-socialist age', *New Left Review*, 1(212), July–August. pp. 68–93.

Freedman, M. (1993) *The Kindness of Strangers: Adult Mentors, Urban Youth and the New Voluntarism*. San Francisco: Jossey-Bass.

Freire, P. (1972) *Pedagogy of the Oppressed*. Harmondsworth: Penguin.

Furlong, A. and Cartmel, C. (2007) *Young People and Social Change. New Perspectives*. Maidenhead: Open University Press.

Gaine, C. (1995) *Still No Problem Here, Anti-Racism in Predominantly White Schools*. Stoke on Trent: Trentham.

Geldard, D. and Geldard, K. (1999) *Counselling Adolescents: The Pro-active Approach*. London: Sage.

Gibson, A. and Davies, B. (1967) *The Social Education of the Adolescent*. London: Routledge & Kegan Paul.

Gilchrist, R. and Jeffs, T. (eds) (2001) *Settlements, Social Changes and Community Action*. London: Jessica Kingsley.

Gilchrist, R., Jeffs, T. and Spence, J. (2003) *Architects of Change: Studies in the History of Community and Youth Work*. Leicester: National Youth Agency.

Gilchrist, R., Jeffs, T. and Spence, J. (2006) *Drawing on the Past: Essays in the History of Community and Youth Work*. Leicester: National Youth Agency.

Gilligan, C. (1982) *In a Different Voice: Psychological Theory and Women's Development*. Cambridge, MA and London: Harvard University Press.

Gilroy, P. (1993) *The Black Atlantic: Modernity and Double Consciousness*. London and New York: Verso.

Goetschius, G. and Tash, J. (1967) *Working with Unattached Youth. Problem, Approach, Method*. London: Routledge and Kegan Paul.

Gramsci, A. (1971) *Selections from the Prison Notebooks*. London: Lawrence & Wishart.

Green, M. and Christian, C. (1998) *Accompanying Young People on the Spiritual Path*. London: The National Society/Church House.

Griffin, C. (1993) *Representations of Youth: The Study of Youth and Adolescence in Britain and America*. Cambridge: Polity.

Griffin, C. (2004) 'Representations of the Young', in Roche et al. (eds), *Youth in Society*. London: Sage.

Hahn, K. (1965) Harrogate address on Outward Bound www. kurthahn.org/writings

Hall, S. (1990) 'Cultural Identity and Diaspora', in Rutherford, (ed.), *Identity: Community, Culture, Difference* London: Lawrence & Wishart.

Hall, S. (2000) 'Conclusion: the multicultural question', in Hannibal-Paci, C. (2002) *Un/settled Multiculturalisms: Diasporas, Entanglements, Transruptions*. Durham, NC: Duke University Press.

Hall, S. and Jefferson, T. (eds) (1976) *Resistance through Rituals: Youth Subcultures in Postwar Britain*. London: Hutchinson.

Hannibal-Paci, C. (2002) *Un/settled Multiculturalisms: Diasporas, Entanglements, Transruptions*. Durham, NC: Duke University Press.

Haraway, D. (1991a) 'A Cyborg manifesto', in *Simians, Cyborgs and Women: The Reinvention of Nature*. London: Free Association Books.

Haraway, D. (1991b) 'Reading Buci Emeceta', in *Simians, Cyborgs and Women: The Reinvention of Nature*. London: Free Association Books.

Harrison, R. and Wise, C. (2005) *Working with Young People*. London: Sage.

Hart, R. (1992) *Children's Participation from Tokenism to Citizenship*. Florence: Innocenti Research Centre.

Haug, F. (1987) *Female Sexualisation: Memory, Work and Politics*. London: Verso.

Hawkins, P. and Shohet, R. (2003) *Supervision in the Helping Professions*. Maidenhead: Open University Press.

Hebdige, D. (1979) *Subculture: The Meaning of Style*. London: Methuen.

Hebdige, D. (1988) *Hiding in the Light: On Images and Things*. London: Comedia.

Henderson, S., Holland, J., McGrellis, S., Sharpe, S. and Thomson, R. (2007) *Inventing Adulthoods: A Biographical Approach to Youth Transitions*. London: Sage.

Hewitt, R. (1986) *White Talk, Black Talk: Inter-racial Friendship and Communication among Adolescents*. London: Cambridge University Press.

HMI (2001) *Youth Work with People with Disabilities*. London: DES.

Hodgson, L. (2004) 'Manufactured civil society: counting the cost', *Critical Social Policy*, 24(2): 139–64.

Home Office (2001) *Community Cohesion A Report of the Independent Review Team chaired by Ted Cantle* (The Cantle Report). London: Stationery Office.

hooks, b. (1993) *Sisters of the Yam: Black Women and Self-Recovery*. Boston, MA: South End Press.

hooks, b. (1994) *Teaching to Transgress: Education as the Practice of Freedom*. London and New York: Routledge.

Howson, C. and Sallah, M. (2007) *Working with Black Young People*. Lyme Regis: Russell House Press.

Hunt, R. and Jensen, J. (2007) *The School Report: The Experiences of Young Gay People in Britain's Schools*. London: Stonewall.

Issitt, M. (2000) 'Critical professionals and reflective practice: the experience of women practitioners in health, welfare and education', in Batsleer, J. and Humphries, B. (eds), *Welfare, Exclusion and Political Agency*. London: Routledge.

Jeffs, T. and Smith, M. (eds) (1987) *Youth Work*. London: Macmillan.

Jeffs, T. and Smith, M. (eds) (1988) *Young People, Inequality and Youth Work*. London: Macmillan.

Jeffs, T. and Smith, M.K. (1996a) *Informal Education – Conversation, Democracy and Learning*. Derby: Education Now Publishing Co-op.

Jeffs, T. and Smith, M. (1996b) 'Getting the dirtbags off the street: curfews and other solutions to juvenile crime', *Youth and Policy*, 52: 1–14.

Jeffs, T. and Smith M.K. (2002) 'Individualisation and Youth Work', *Youth and Policy*, 76: 39–65.

Jeffs, T. and Smith, M.K. (2006) 'Where is Youth Matters taking us?' *Youth and Policy*, 91: 23–40.

John, G. (1981) *In the Service of Black Youth. A Study of the Political Culture of Youth and Community Work with Black People in English Cities*. Leicester: National Association of Youth Clubs.

John, G. (2006) *Taking a Stand: Gus John Speaks on Education, Race, Social Action and Civil Unrest*. Manchester: Gus John Partnership.

Jones, G. (2002). *The Youth Divide: Diverging Paths to Adulthood*. York: Joseph Rowntree Foundation.

Joseph Rowntree Foundation (2006) *What Will it Take to End Child Poverty? Findings July 2006*. York: JRF.

Khan, M.G. (ed.) (2006) Special issue on Muslim youth work, *Youth and Policy*, Summer.

Kirkby, P. and Bryson, S. (2002) *Measuring the Magic? Evaluating and Researching Young People's Participation in Public Decision Making*. London: Carnegie Young Persons' Initiative.

Kitzinger, C. and Wilkinson, S. (1995) 'Transitions from heterosexuality to lesbianism: The discursive production of lesbian identities', *Developmental Psychology*, 31: 95–104.

Ledwith, M. and Asgill, P. (2000) 'Critical alliance: Black and white women working together for social justice', *Community Development Journal* 35(3): 290.

Lees, S. (1983) *Losing Out: Sexuality and Adolescent Girls*. London: Hutchinson.

Levitas, R. (2004) *The Inclusive Society? Social Exclusion and New Labour*. Basingstoke: Palgrave Macmillan.

Lister, R., Smith, N., Middleton, S. and Cox, L. (2005) 'Young people and citizenship', in Barry, M. (ed.), *Youth Policy and Social Inclusion: Critical Debate with Young People*. London: Routledge.

Local Government Association (2006) *Children in Trouble*. London: LGA Report.

Lorenz, W. (1994) *Social Work in a Changing Europe*. London: Routledge.

Luxmoore, N. (2000) *Listening to Young People in School, Youth Work and Counselling*. London: Jessica Kingsley.

Matthews, R. and Young, J. (eds) (2003) *The New Politics of Crime and Punishment*. Devon: Willan.

McDonald, R. and Marsh, J. (2005) *Disconnected Youth? Growing Up in Britain's Poor Neighbourhoods*. Basingstoke: Palgrave.

McPherson, W. (1999) *The Stephen Lawrence Inquiry*. Cm 4262–I. London: Home Office.

Memmi, A. (1965) *The Colonizer and the Colonized*. New York: Orion Press.

Mental Health Foundation (1999) *Bright Futures: Promoting Children and Young People's Mental Health*. London: Mental Health Foundation.

Merton, B. et al. (2004) *An Evaluation of the Impact of Youth Work in England*. Nottingham: DFES.

Miles, S., Pohl, A., Stauber, B. and Walther, A. (2002) *Communities of Youth: Cultural Practice and Informal Learning*. Aldershot: Ashgate.

Milner, M. (1986) *A Life of One's Own*. London: Virago.

Mistry, T. and Brown, A. (1991) 'Black/white co-working in groups', *Groupwork*, 4 (2): 18–24.

Moss, B. (2005) *Religion and Spirituality*. Lyme Regis: Russell House Press.

NAPO (2005) *Asbos: An Analysis of the First Six Years*. London: NAPO (July).

Nussbaum, M. (1999) *Sex and Social Justice*. Oxford: Oxford University Press.

Nussbaum, M. and Sen, A. (1993) *The Quality of Life*. Oxford: Clarendon Press.

Oakley, A. (2004–5) 'The researcher's agenda for evidence', in What Kind of Evidence Does Government need? Special issue of *Evaluation and Research in Education*, 18 (1 & 2): 12–27.

Oldfield, C. and Fowler, C. (2004) *Mapping Children and Young People's Participation in England*. Dfes Research Report 584. London: DFES.

Ord, J. (2004) 'The youth work curriculum and the transforming Youth Work agenda', *Youth and Policy*, 83: 43–60.

Ord, J (2007) *Youth Work Process, Product and Practice: Creating an Authentic Curriculum in Work with Young People*. Lyme Regis: Russell House.

Palmer, S. (2002) *Multicultural Counselling. A Reader*. London: Sage.

Perrin, J. (2006) *The Climbing Essays*. Edinburgh: Neil Wilson.

Phillips, A. (1993) *On Kissing, Tickling and Being Bored*. London: Faber.

Pierson, J. and Smith, J. (2001) *Rebuilding Communities: Common Problems and Approaches*. Basingstoke: Palgrave.

Piper, D. E. (2007) *Young People, Suicide and Self-Harm*. Brighton: TSA.

Richardson, L. D. and Wolfe, M. (eds) (2001) *Principles and Practice of Informal Education: Learning through Life*. Falmer: Routledge.

Roche, J. (2004) 'Children's rights participation and dialogue' in Roche, J. Tucker, S. Thomson, R. and Flynn, R., *Youth in Society*. London: Sage.

Roche, J., Tucker, S., Thomson, R. and Flynn, R. (2004) *Youth in Society*. London: Sage.

Rose, N. (1996) *Inventing Ourselves: Psychology, Power and Personhood*. New York and Cambridge: Cambridge University Press.

Roy, A. (2002) Sydney Peace Prize Lecture http://www.smh.com.au.

Rutherford, J. (ed.) (1990) *Identity: Community, Culture, Difference*. London: Lawrence & Wishart.

Salamensky, S. I. (ed.) (2001) *Talk, Talk, Talk: The Cultural life of Everyday Conversation*. London: Routledge.

Sawbridge, M and Spence, J. (1991) *The Dominance of the Male Agenda in Community and Youth Work*. Durham: Durham University Press.

Scott, J. (1990) *Domination and the Arts of Resistance*. New Haven and London: Yale University Press.

Sen, A. (1999) *Development as Freedom*. Oxford: Oxford University Press.

Sennett, R. (2003) *Respect in a World of Inequality*. New York: Norton.

Smith, M. (1988) *Developing Youth Work*. Milton Keynes: Open University Press.

Smith, M. (1993) *Local Education: Community, Conversation, Praxis*. Maidenhead: Open University Press.

Smith, M. E. and Smith, M. K. (2002) 'Friendship: theory and experience', in *The Encyclopaedia of Informal Education*. www.infed.org/encyclopaedia.htm

Smithson, H. and Flint, J. (2006) 'Responding to young people's involvement in anti-social behaviour: a study of local initiatives in Manchester and Glasgow', *Youth and Policy*, 93 Autumn: 21–39.

Social Exclusion Unit (1999) *Teenage Pregnancy*. Cm 4342. London: The Stationery Office.

Spandler, H. and Warner, S. (2007) *Beyond Fear and Control: Working with Young People Who Self-harm*. Manchester: 42nd Street.

Spence, J. (2006) 'Working with girls and young women: a broken history', in Gilchrist, R., Jeffs, T. and Spence, J. *Drawing on the Past: Essays in the History of Communty and Youth Work*. Leicester: National Youth Agency.

Spence, J. and Devanney, C. (2007) *Youth Work: Voices of Practice*. Leicester: National Youth Agency.

Stratford, E. (2002) 'On the edge: a tale of skaters and urban governance', *Social and Cultural Geography*, 3(2): 193–204.

Tate, S. (2005) *Black Skins, Black Masks: Hybridity, Dialogism, Performativity*. London: Ashgate.

Thomas, P. (2003) 'Young people, community cohesion and the role of youth work in building social capital', *Youth and Policy*, 81: 41–60.

Thomas, T. (2005) 'The continuing story of the ASBO', *Youth and Policy*, 87 (Spring): 5–14.

Thomas, T. (2007) 'A year of tackling anti-social behaviour: some reflections on realities and rhetoric', *Youth and Policy*, 94 (Winter): 5–19.

Thompson, K. (1998) *Moral Panics*. London and New York: Routledge.

Thompson, N. (ed.) (2002) *Loss and Grief: A Guide for Human Service Practitioners*. Basingstoke: Palgrave.

Tronto, J. (1993) *Moral Boundaries: A Political Argument for an Ethic of Care*. London: Routledge.

UNICEF Report Card Seven (2007) *Child Poverty in Perspective: An Overview of Child Wellbeing in Rich Countries*. Florence: UNICEF.

Valentine, G. (2004) *Public Space and the Culture of Childhood*. London: Ashgate.

Walkerdine, V., Lucey, H. and Melody, J. (2002) *Growing up Girl: Psychosocial Explorations of Gender and Class*. Basingstoke: Macmillan Palgrave.

Webb, M. (2001) 'Working with Black young people', in Factor, F. et al., *The RHP Companion to Working with Young People*. Lyme Regis: Russell House.

Wetherell, M. and Potter, J. (1992) *Mapping the Language of Racism*. Hemel Hempstead: Harvester Wheatsheaf.

Williams, L.O. (1988) *Partial Surrender: Race and Resistance in the Youth Service*. Basingstoke: Falmer Press.

Williams, R. (2004) *Silence and Honey Cakes*. Oxford: Lion.

Willis, P. (1990) *Common Culture*. Buckingham: Open University Press.

Wilson, R. (2006) *What Works for Reconciliation?* Belfast: Democratic Dialogue.

Winnicott, D.W. (1964) *The Child, the Family and the Outside World*. London: Penguin.

Winnicott, D.W. (1971) *Playing and Reality*. London: Tavistock.

Wolfe, M. (2001) 'Conversation', in Richardson, L.D. and Wolfe, M. (eds), *Principles and Practice of Informal Education: Learning Through Life*. London: Routledge. pp. 124–37.

Woolley, H. and Johns, R. (2001) 'Skateboarding: the city as playground', *Journal of Urban Design*, 6(2): 211–30.

Young, I. M. (2000) *Inclusion and Democracy*. Oxford Political Theory Series. Oxford: OUP.

Young, K. (1999) 'The youth worker as guide, philosopher and friend', in Banks, S. (ed.), *Ethical Issues in Youth Work*. London: Routledge.

Young, K. (2006) *The Art of Youth Work*. Lyme Regis: Russell House.

Index